A Scout's Book
OF
Signs, Signals
and Symbols

THE PICTURE ROCK BY THE TRAIL

THESE SYMBOLS SIGNIFY:

Easy two miles to good camp, plenty of food and good water, horses, boats, and a jolly time

A Scout's Book

— OF —

Signs, Signals and Symbols

Daniel Beard

Illustrated by the Author

Dover Publications, Inc.
Mineola, New York

Bibliographical Note

This Dover edition, first published in 2018, is an unabridged republication of the work originally published by J. B. Lippincott Company, Philadelphia, in 1918, under the title *The American Boys' Book of Signs, Signals and Symbols.*

International Standard Book Number

ISBN-13: 978-0-486-82086-6
ISBN-10: 0-486-82086-6

Manufactured in the United States by LSC Communications
82086601   2018
www.doverpublications.com

PREFACE

FOR years the writer has been working on these ideographs, picturegraphs, tramps,' yeggmen's, scouts,' trappers,' gypsies' and Indian signs, symbols and signals, not with the object of writing a cumbersome, more or less accurate, dictionary, but for the purpose of selecting such systems of signs as may be of use to the boys in their games in the open. Especially are these cryptograms, hieroglyphics, cabalistic figures and emblems useful to our youthful army of Boy Scouts and it is for them particularly that this book was written, although now that war is declared it is hoped that some hints herein may be of service to the fighting men of our country.

The desire to be of help to our great nation in everything he does for boys prompted the author to rewrite and enlarge this whole book after it was in the hands of the publishers. This made it necessary to postpone its publication for a year. Weather signs and animal signs have been added because of the demand for them from the boys themselves.

DANIEL CARTER BEARD

FLUSHING, L. I.
MAY 1, 1918

CONTENTS

CHAPTER   PAGE

I. SIGNS OF DIRECTION............................... 17

II. WILDERNESS SIGNS OF DIRECTION...................... 21

III. CHALK-SIGNS FOR COMMAND AND INFORMATION............ 27

IV. DANGER SIGNS....................................... 35

V. DANGER NAUTICAL................................... 40

VI. TRAIL SIGNS FOR DANGER, CAUTION, CALAMITY AND CRIES
IN THE WILDERNESS FOR HELP...................... 44

VII. SIGNS OF GOOD LUCK................................ 48

VIII. WORD SIGNS.. 51

IX. MAP SIGNS OF PEOPLE............................... 54

X. CHALK- AND MAP-SIGNS OF ANIMALS................... 57

XI. SIGNS OF INANIMATE OR MOTIONLESS THINGS............ 60

XII. SIGNS OF THE ELEMENTS............................ 64

XIII. CELESTIAL SIGNS................................... 67

XIV. SIGNS OF COLOR................................... 69

XV. SIGNS OF THE SEASONS AND SIGNS OF TIME.............. 77

XVI. SECRET WRITING—THE CABALLA...................... 83

XVII. NUMERALS OF THE MAGIC........................... 91

XVIII. GESTURE SIGNALS.................................. 97

XIX. COMMON GESTURE LANGUAGE.......................... 105

XX. HAND ALPHABETS, DEAF AND DUMB ALPHABETS.......... 112

XXI. SIGNAL CODES..................................... 123

XXII. BELL, ROPE AND WHISTLE RAILWAY SIGNALS............ 145

XXIII. RAILROAD, HAND-FLAG, LANTERN RAILWAY SIGNALS...... 148

XXIV. STEAMER TOOT TALK............................... 162

XXV. WEATHER SIGNS.................................... 173

XXVI. WEATHER SIGNS.................................... 187

XXVII. FLAGS—THE RED, WHITE AND BLUE................... 206

XXVIII. FOLLOWING THE CHANGES IN THE FLAG................ 218

XXIX. LIBERTY POLES.................................... 233

XXX. SIGNS SHOWN BY TRAILS, TRACKS, TRACES AND SPOOR OF
ANIMALS....................................... 242

SIGNS, SIGNALS AND SYMBOLS

INTRODUCTION

THE Goddess of Liberty is a sign or symbol representing no real person or god, but she does represent the idea of human freedom. Columbia in a like manner represents America as Britannia does Great Britain. The Bear is the totem, or sign, of Russia, the Bald-headed Eagle the totem of United States.

AMERICAN GUMPTION

It takes gumption to really understand these things, and the American boy is supposed to possess a large amount of this article in his make-up; in fact, this is supposed to be also true of the American man. Gumption is a good old-fashioned word which implies a multitude of virtues. Brother Jonathan himself typifies gumption, that is, he stands for and is the sign of gumption. But how many of my readers know who is Brother Jonathan?

Brother Jonathan has been neglected lately and Uncle Sam has usurped his place in our newspaper and magazine cartoons, but the two characters are not one and the same person. Brother Jonathan represents the whole of the American people put through the melting pot and moulded into one person. Brother Jonathan *is the people* and *not the government*, he is the symbol of democracy.

Uncle Sam represents the machine of the government, or the organized power used to govern our nation.

Of course, here in America where the people govern

11

themselves, one is apt to mix these two characters. But there is just the same difference between Uncle Sam and Brother Jonathan as there is between the King and the people, or the King of England and John Bull. The King may represent the people and may not; for instance, John Bull may discharge the King at any time but the King could never discharge John Bull. Remember that both John Bull and Brother Jonathan represent the peoples of their respective countries, and that Uncle Sam and the crown represent the governments, and all of these imaginary persons are signs and symbols representing ideas.

Pioneers, trappers, surveyors, hunters, fishermen, and boys, as well as all the vagabonds of the road, including the hoboes, tramps, yeggmen, gypsies, and the American Indians, all have a system of trail signs—picturegraphs, ideographs, ciphers and hieroglyphics, with meanings understood by the initiated. Recently the automobilists have added their contribution to the road signs, and the great usefulness of all these signs lies in the fact that if one understands the symbol, one does not need to understand the language of the sign-maker.

For instance, if the traveler sees on a rock by the side of the trail or a fence, or on a barn by the roadside, the sign of danger, no matter what tongue is used by the traveler he knows that he must proceed with caution, for that sign spells danger in every language; it is a symbol representing the idea of danger.

The author has made no attempt to invent a system of signs, for the very good reason that there are signs already in use, some of which have stood the test of centuries, and the collection in this book is made up from such recognized systems and is used either in their original form or in combination with one of the other original systems.

Almost all the trail signs of the open are taken from the American Indian and the American Buckskin men, and also almost all of the signs indicating natural phenomena, such as rain, cloud, water, day, night, month, etc., are taken directly from the Indians.

The poetry of the Indians' minds is displayed in their symbols as well as in their figurative language, which, for instance, has no such word as "merry," but designates that state of mind most beautifully by calling it sunshine in the heart.

But most of the chalk-signs, such as are used on fences, barns, and sign-posts are cribbed from the "Knights of the Road," in other words from hoboes and tramps, and are more sordid in their meanings than those of the white trappers or red Indians. The signs indicating color are taken from heraldry.

It was no small task to secure the vagabonds' secret symbols and their meaning; they were picked up one by one and verified as the opportunity occurred, for they are especially guarded secrets among the vagabonds and it is hoped that the publishing of them and making them free to all will accomplish two purposes, one in supplying a useful system of road signs to the hunters, fishermen, Boy Scouts and other pedestrians, and the other in defeating the purposes of the underworld by robbing these signs of their secrecy.

A householder, finding the tramp sign of the easy mark on his house, may erase the same and substitute the danger mark, and the Boy Scout, the pedestrian, the hunter and the fisherman may use the easy mark to show the easy trail and the danger mark to show the dangerous trail. Besides which all sorts of useful information may be conveyed by one patrol of scouts to those following by the use of a few chalk-marks on a board fence or sidewalk. By putting the sign of the past, then the sign of direction, then the sign of noon and the sign of scout drawn across the wavy line of direction, one will see that a Boy Scout passed here at noon. If necessary, a long letter or communication may be written by the use of the signs here given, a letter which will be much shorter than written words.

PICTUREGRAPH LETTER RECEIVED BY THE AUTHOR FROM A HUNTING FRIEND THEN IN THE WILDS OF THE PEACE RIVER COUNTRY

The angular line at the top of the letter represents mountains. The first animal to the left is a goat we know from its straight horns, breeches and peglike feet. Underneath that is a caribou, which we know from the shape of its horns. Underneath that is another caribou. To the right, lying on its back, is a bear. Underneath that is another bear with claws, which must be a grizzly bear. At the bottom the canoe is cached with paddles under it. The man has a pack on his back and a gun on his shoulder and is making tracks toward the right. Over his head is his totem, which tells who he is. There is a dotted line to where the man appears again, saluting another man. In front of the man with the gun are five suns. This would indicate that it will be five days before the man has finished the dotted line. The animals all being on their backs tell us that they are dead and it all reads, "I have been hunting in the mountains. I bagged one rocky mountain goat, two caribou, one black bear, and one grizzly bear. I have cached my canoe and started home. I will see you in five days."

The author has taken the liberty of discarding many signs with the same meaning as that of other signs in the same system and adopting such as seemed to correspond with a general universal system. This must not be understood to mean that but one sign, for instance, for danger, is retained; on the contrary, we give the flag-sign, the chalk-sign, the trail-sign and the wilderness sign for danger, but we do not duplicate these in the same system.

CHAPTER I

SIGNS OF DIRECTION

As Found on Sign-posts and as Marked with Pencil or Chalk on Fences, Barns, Sheds and Telephone Poles

The signs of direction may be divided into two general families; the first is composed of painted sign-posts and chalk-marks used in the more settled parts of the community and the second is made up of what might be termed the wilderness signs of direction. In this second family are included trappers,' voyagers,' Indians' and gypsy signs made of the material found in the wilderness, the trails or the road.

Everyone should be familiar enough with these signs to read and use them intelligently. For instance, Fig. 1 is the traffic sign adopted by cities in order to prevent the streets from becoming blockaded; this is simple and explains itself; it is a command for all vehicles to take the direction in which the arrow points. But there are other signs here given, which are understood by few people. For instance, Fig. 6, which is a chalk or pencil sign used by yeggmen and hoboes to warn comrades that they must hit the trail and disappear as quickly as possible. Many a house-holder might avoid serious inconvenience, if not disaster, by becoming familiar with such signs and using them to their own advantage in place of allowing the under-world and enemies of society to monopolize their use. With boys, these signs suggest all sorts of games of trailing and searching for hidden treasure and open a vast field of new sports.

17

Signs of Direction
Sign-post and Chalk-signs

1

Fig. 1. White arrow in parallelogram cutting a circle horizontally. Go this way only. (Traffic sign.)

THIS WAY.

2

THIS WAY.

Fig. 2. Hand with index finger pointing, or an arrow. Usually on painted signs and maps indicating that the proper direction is that indicated by the point of the arrow or the pointing finger. (Sign-boards.)

3

NO USE GOING THIS WAY.

Fig. 3. An arrow with a circle on its shaft means literally "nothing doing" in this direction. (Hobo and wilderness Scout Sign.)

4

I WENT THIS WAY.

Fig. 4. Arrow with a perpendicular line across the shaft indicates that the leading man, scout or person left the beaten trail at point marked and took the direction indicated by the arrow. Both Figures 3 and 4 are used on explorers' and military maps. (Wilderness Scout Sign.)

5

CONCEALED NOTE
3 PACES THIS WAY.

Fig. 5. An arrow with a parallelogram where the feathers should be, tells the reader that a message, a letter, or a document of some kind is concealed three paces from the sign in the direction indicated by the arrow. (English Boy Scout Sign.)

Fig. 6. Circle with two arrows across it is a command to move on quickly. A chalk-sign used by hoboes, yeggmen and vagabonds. Usually a warning that the constable or police are looking for them. (Tramp Sign.)

Fig. 7. Circle with dash cutting the circumference. Used at crossroads. Means take the trail pointed to by the line. (Hobo sign.)

Fig. 8. The letter V placed horizontally is really the outline of an arrow-head with the same meaning as the pointing hand and the arrow. (Fig. 2.) A sign of direction.

Fig. 9. Is the same as Fig. 8 but you will note it has a short line near its point, or apex. This means that camp or the place of rendezvous is but a short distance ahead in the direction indicated. (Modification of Indian Stick sign.)

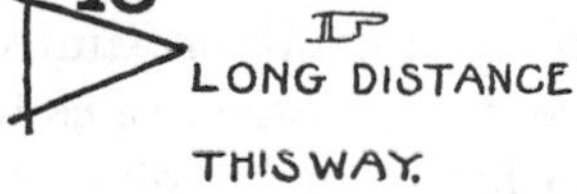

Fig. 10. The same as Figure 9 but in this case the vertical line is at the open wide part of the V in place of at the point. Meaning a long distance to camp. (Adapted from the Indian Trail signs.)

11

5 MILES THIS WAY.

Fig. 11. The same as the preceding figures but with an addition of a number of vertical lines crossing the V. With the Indians each vertical line stands for a day's journey, but with the people in the more thickly settled country, distances are measured by miles, and each line indicates a mile. With boys using these chalk-signs in town, each line will represent a block or city square. (Adapted from Indian Trail signs.)

12

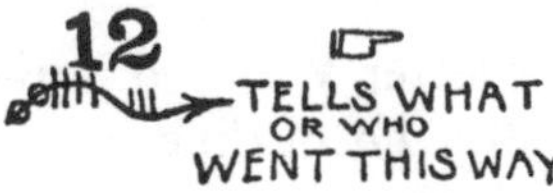

TELLS WHAT OR WHO WENT THIS WAY.

Fig. 12. A wave stem arrow with circles, cross lines and half lines. Is used by the knights of the road, gypsies, tramps and hoboes to tell their fellows in this case, that two children, four men and three women passed this way. The arrow indicates direction, the circles indicate children, the four lines crossing the shaft of the arrow indicate men and the three half lines indicate women, which tells us very distinctly that in the underworld children are looked upon as ciphers, and women as but half men. (European Hobo sign.)

The foregoing signs of direction may be pencilled, marked with a soft brick, a burnt stick or a piece of chalk or painted on signposts. But, as a rule, they are not practical signs to use in a country where there are no fences or buildings or sidewalks, consequently the people traversing the wilderness and wild country resort to other methods of marking the trail.

CHAPTER II

WILDERNESS SIGNS OF DIRECTION

On Indian Trails; Game Trails and Prospectors' Trails; Also Used by Gypsies, Scouts, Explorers and Sportsmen

WHEN the trees blanketed our continent from the Atlantic Ocean to the Mississippi River with a dark and gloomy forest in which there were only occasional openings, or prairies like those which existed in Indiana and Illinois, it was necessary to mark the trails through the woods in order that one should not become lost. True, the country was traversed by Big Game trails, war-paths and Indian trails then known as "traces." But many of these, even the celebrated war-paths, were overgrown with underbrush and weeds so as to be only distinguishable to the initiated and accomplished wilderness man. Hence when the white men came, they marked roads for the settlers. The surveyors and pioneers did this by blazes made with their axes on the tree trunks. These were called blazed trails, "*cantiagge*," marked trees, by the Long Island Indians and they are still used in the North woods, in Maine, in the wilderness of Canada and the far North, as well as in the few forests remaining in the West.

The blazed trail is either made by chipping pieces of bark off the side of the trees along the line of travel, known as "Go by" blazes (surveyors' marks), or by what is called a "spot-trail," *i.e.*, by making big blazes on the face of the trees along the line, so that one spot may be seen from any other preceding it.

Fig. 12½. Three blazes on a tree indicate an important "line" tree, or more frequently a witness tree for a corner of plot of land; usually another blaze is made on side of tree nearest the stake or stone marking the corner.

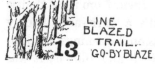

Fig. 13. Blazed trail. It tells the traveler that a line or trail runs alongside of the points marked. It does not give the particular direction like the arrow because this trail may be followed either way. In the diagram the blazes are much closer than they would be in the wilderness, but it is so made that the reader may more readily understand it. (Surveyors,' trappers,' foresters,' and explorers' sign.)

Fig. 14. Spot trail; useful in traveling after sunset as one blaze may be seen from a position close to any other blaze, but cannot be seen from a position to one side of it. (Hunters,' trappers and foresters' signs.) With surveyors a spot mark indicates a line tree, that is a tree standing on the line; sometimes both a spot and a side blaze is used to show that the line hits the tree on one side.

Fig. 15. Broken bush trails. When traveling in an unknown country, one bends and breaks the bushes backwards so that their tops point backwards. When retracing one's steps, one's eyes will catch the exposed under surface of the leaves on the broken bushes, thus making it easy to find the way back. (Hunters,' trappers,' and Scout signs.)

Fig. 16. (*Kikaige*, I make marks on the road setting up branches—Chippewa). When a stick is stuck diagonally in the ground, the free point shows the direction to camp. In the Northwest, when an Indian has made a kill of moose, sheep or caribou he puts one end of a fresh willow stick in the ground and wraps a bit of the skin of the dead animal on the end of it as an invitation to anyone coming along that trail to come and eat. If the willow stick is fresh and not withered the traveler knows that food and camp are not far ahead of him, but if the willow stick is wilted and drooping, the traveler knows that it has been there a long time and the hunters have probably eaten up the food supply and hit the trail; but the stick in Fig. 16 simply indicates direction. (Abnaki Indians.)

Fig. 17. A long upright stick at the upper end of the pointer tells us that camp is a long distance ahead. (Abnaki Indians.)

Fig. 18. A short upright stick near the buried end of the pointer tells us that camp is a short distance ahead. (Abnaki Indians.)

Fig. 19. A number of upright sticks against the leaning stick indicate the number of "sleeps," or days' journey (for the Indian), but with the Boy Scouts of America it tells the number of miles to camp. (Abnaki Indians.)

Fig. 20. A cleft stick with a forked stick in the cleft tells us that the direction is pointed by the end of the stick. (Gypsy sign.) A green stick thrust in the mud near the shore of a lake or stream, with a chip in the cleft at the top shows the canoe trail. This is sometimes blazed on side and front to show direction taken by outgoing canoe party. (N. W. Quebec Indians.)

Fig. 21. A stone on top of another stone tells us that this is the trail.

Fig. 22. A stone with another stone on top of it and a stone to the right means to turn to the right. (English Boy Scout Sign.)

Fig. 23. The same with a stone to the left of it reads; "Turn to the left here." (English Boy Scout Sign.)

Fig. 24. In the prairie and open country a bunch of grass tied together at the top tells us that this is the trail. (Sioux Indian Sign, Dr. Eastman.)

Fig. 25. If the top ends of the grass are bent to the right, it tells us to turn to the right. (Sioux Indian Sign, Dr. Eastman.)

Fig. 26. If the top of the grass is bent to the left, it tells one to turn to the left. (Sioux Indian Sign. Dr. Eastman.)

Fig. 27. Two sticks laid on the ground in the form of a "V," indicate the direction same as Fig. 8. (Gypsies.)

Fig. 28. A row of little stones laid in the form of a "V" indicates the direction taken. (Gypsies.)

Fig. 29. A green forked stick laid with apparent carelessness upon the ground to the keen eye of the vagabond tells him that companions have lately passed in this direction. (Gypsies.)

30

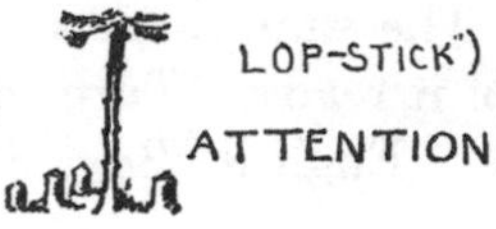

LOP-STICK

ATTENTION!

Fig. 30. The lop-stick. In heavily wooded districts when the attention of a passer-by is required, a prominent tree is selected, a space cleared around it and the branches of the tree lopped off for a considerable distance up the trunk. Such a mark cannot escape the eye of the passer-by. (Alaska Prospectors, Explorers, and Indians.)

If, for instance, one of a party goes ahead and comes to a lake which is crossed, the water affords no means of marking a trail, but if on the hill or high bank where he again takes up his trail, a tree is lopped in this manner, it will attract the immediate attention of those following and enable them to pick up the trail on the opposite side of the lake. The lop-stick is frequently made to commemorate some event:

"The next day we dug him a grave above high-water mark. . . . I climbed the tree to make a memorial of the North—the lop-stick."— STEFANSON.

The lop-stick in the wilderness of Canada, now 1918, is frequently a wireless station used probably for war purposes. Several such trees were recently pointed out to the author by wilderness canoe men.

CHAPTER III

For the Wayfarer, Pedestrian, Bicyclist, Motor Cyclist or the Automobilist

A Call for Help

The illustration shows a village fence with an important chalk message on it. In the illustration the chalk message

is about fifty times bigger in proportion to the fence than it really would be when the boys make it. But we had to enlarge it so that it would show in the cut. By referring to the

27

diagram (Fig. 41) we see that three (3) is a call for help and in Fig. 97 we see that the skull and crossbones stand for a doctor, the spiral sign with an arrow point on one end of it (Fig. 33) is a command that means "come." The next one, a circle with two arrows (Fig. 6) reads "Hit the trail double quick." The next one is the Indian sign for lightning (Fig. 149). The lightning is striking a rude drawing of a powder horn (Fig. 98) which stands for a Scout. The next with two intersecting parallelograms (Fig. 79) stands for timidity, alarm, afraid. The next one is the sign of direction (Figs. 9, 10, 11) and tells us that camp is two miles in the direction pointed and the next one is the tent which means "camp," indicating that it is two miles to camp. Putting these meanings together, the message would read, "Help, a doctor wanted. Come double quick. One of our scouts has been shocked by lightning and we are afraid of the consequences. It is two miles in this direction to camp."

In towns and cities where paved streets or sidewalks offer the opportunity, chalk-signs are particularly handy. But minute pencil signs will answer the purpose for the Boy Scouts as they often do for the hoboes.

Almost every telegraph pole, water tank and similar roadside object is utilized by the vagabonds as a sign-board on which they scribble their queer symbols, and such telegraph poles are just as handy for Boy Scouts as they are for outlaws and may be used by the boys without disfiguring the poles, for the little lead pencil symbol will not be seen by any one except those looking for them.

Each patrol of scouts should, of course, sign its message with the patrol totem no matter how rudely drawn the animal may be.

Fishermen, automobilists, sportsmen or military scouts may upon occasions find it particularly handy to use the telephone poles and this system of chalk or pencil ideographs to convey information to others of their party, and if the messages are signed with some recognized totem or initials, there will be no mistake made by those following the trail. Of course it should be understood that the trail followers should look for information at certain designated places, otherwise they must look for messages at the most likely places where such messages might be written.

CHALK-SIGNS OF COMMAND AND INFORMATION FOR THE TRAIL

31 PERSEVERE. Fig. 31. Two rude circles intersecting each other is a command to persevere, never say die, don't give up. (Hobo.)

32 GO! MARCH ON! Fig. 32. Circle with arrow. Command to go. (Hobo.)

33 COME! Fig. 33. A spiral with arrow point to left. Command to come to camp, to come back. (Boy Pioneers.)

34 HALT! Fig. 34. A sign taken by vagabonds from the ancient books of magic, a command to stop, to halt. Stop! (Hobo.)

35 HOLD YOUR TONGUE! Fig. 35. A diamond admonishes you to keep quiet, hold your tongue. (Hobo.)

36 BE GOOD! Fig. 36. A cross. A hint to be good. With tramps this means, give them a religious talk and they will give you food. (Tramp.)

37 ⊤ or ⋊ WORK FOR FOOD

38 ⊔ YOU MAY CAMP HERE.

39 ⫟ YOU MAY SLEEP IN HAY LOFT HERE.

40 △△△△ TELL YOUR STORY.

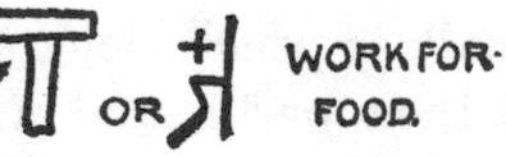

Fig. 37. Two signs taken from ancient book of magic and used by tramps to tell where they can get food by working for it. (Hobo.)

Fig. 38. You may camp here. (Hobo sign.) From the letter Teth celestial writing, magic.

Fig. 39. Tells you that you may sleep in the hay loft. Probably taken from ancient magic. (Hobo.)

Fig. 40. Among the tramps and vagabonds this means to tell a pitiful story and you will excite the sympathy of your audience. But with the Scouts it simply means to tell your story, that is, make your report. (Hobo.)

The foregoing are characteristic tramp signs, but as anyone may see they also form a useful set of symbols for sportsmen or military officers and will be found particularly useful to Scoutmasters and Boy Scouts on their hikes and in their games. Many of the games being on the order of a paper chase, chalk marks make less litter and mess and tell a more coherent story for the hounds.

Road-signs for Automobiles

Recently the automobilists have adopted some very useful and practical road signs. In the first place they have painted the telephone and telegraph posts with bands of color to mark the roads so colored on the automobile maps, but the real practical road signs consists first of a parabola, which is a term in geometry for a certain curve made by the

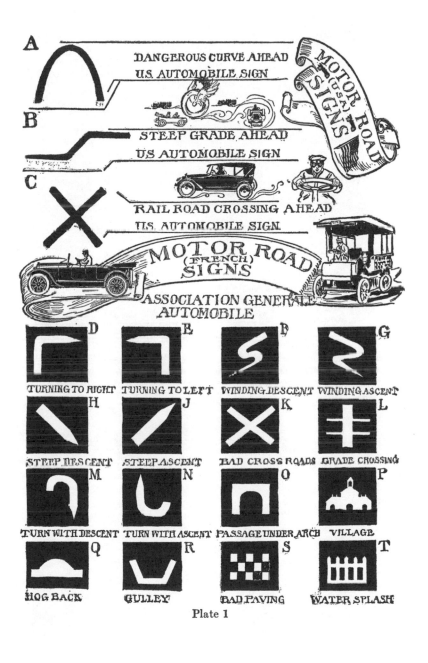

A — DANGEROUS CURVE AHEAD — U.S. AUTOMOBILE SIGN

B — STEEP GRADE AHEAD — U.S. AUTOMOBILE SIGN

C — RAIL ROAD CROSSING AHEAD — U.S. AUTOMOBILE SIGN

MOTOR ROAD (U.S.A.) SIGNS

MOTOR ROAD (FRENCH) SIGNS — ASSOCIATION GENERALE AUTOMOBILE

D — TURNING TO RIGHT	E — TURNING TO LEFT	F — WINDING DESCENT	G — WINDING ASCENT
H — STEEP DESCENT	J — STEEP ASCENT	K — BAD CROSS ROADS	L — GRADE CROSSING
M — TURN WITH DESCENT	N — TURN WITH ASCENT	O — PASSAGE UNDER ARCH	P — VILLAGE
Q — HOG BACK	R — GULLEY	S — BAD PAVING	T — WATER SPLASH

Plate 1

section of a cone. Fig. A (Plate 1). This warns the chauffeur that he is approaching a dangerous curve in the road.

Steep grade ahead is indicated by two straight lines, one a little above the other, joined at the middle ends by a diagonal line, Fig. B (Plate 1), thus showing a profile view of the road with a steep grade to it.

Railroad crossing! look out for the locomotive! is shown by a simple crossing of two lines like a letter X, Fig. C (Plate 1). These signs are very conspicuous on the roads in Connecticut, especially in the neighborhood of Danbury.

Somewhere about 1902 the "Association General Automobile" that is, the French Automobile Society adopted quite an extended series of road signs for the purpose of warning motorists when they approach dangerous grade crossings, cross-roads, villages, steep hills, bad pavements, arches, gullies and hog-backs, or as the French call them, donkey-backs. They also indicate which way the road is turning, when the road turns to the right it is so shown by Fig. D (Plate 1).

Turning to the left is the same sign reversed with the pointed end pointing to the left, Fig. E (Plate 1).

A winding descent is indicated by a rude S-shaped figure tipped up diagonally with the top end pointing to the right, Fig. F (Plate 1).

A winding ascent is indicated by the same sort of S-shaped figure tipped up towards the left, Fig. G (Plate 1).

A steep descent is shown by a bomb set diagonally on the sign with a pointed end aimed towards the right-hand lower corner, Fig. H (Plate 1).

A steep ascent is indicated by the same bomb-shaped figure placed diagonally upon the sign with the pointed end pointing to the upper right-hand corner, Fig. J (Plate 1).

Bad cross-roads is practically the same sign that they use here in America for railroad crossings, Fig. K (Plate 1).

Grade crossing is indicated by a broad band representing the road with two lines crossing it at right angles representing the rails, Fig. L (Plate 1).

A turn in the road going down hill is shown by part of a "U" with the pointed end turning down, Fig. M (Plate 1).

A turn in the road going up hill is a reverse of the last figure with a sharp end pointing up. Fig. N (Plate 1).

Where the road passes under an arch a warning sign of an arch upon the sign-board tells the chauffeur to be careful, Fig. O (Plate 1).

A village is indicated by a couple of crudely drawn houses with a public building in between them; Fig. P (Plate 1).

A donkey-back, or hog-back as we know it in America, is shown by a diagram of that sort of a hill, Fig. Q (Plate 1).

A gulley is indicated by a conventional outline of a gulley. Fig. R (Plate 1).

Bad paving is something all of us would like to know before we hit it, and our machine goes jumping over the stones. The French sign for it is a section of a checkerboard, Fig. S (Plate 1).

The water splash is foretold by the diagram of a fence on the sign-board, Fig. T (Plate 1).

There are many of these French signs which are unnecessary here, in America, as automobile signs, but some of them could be used to advantage on automobile maps and also upon military maps, for in map-making the more simple conventional signs one has the less lettering is necessary, and consequently the more simple and more easily read is the map.

CHAPTER IV

DANGER SIGNS

It is of vital importance to the whole outdoor world that a uniform system of signs should be adopted and understood to indicate trouble, disaster, and a call for help. Owing to the fact that one writer has, through misapprehension or typographical error, given us two shots as a call for help, it has put a dangerous confusion of ideas in many amateurs' minds. It should be recognized among all outdoor people, including hunters, explorers, military men, and Boy Scouts, that THREE OF ANYTHING stands for something serious, for a call for help, for a sign of danger. Three might be called the Paul Revere among the signs, spreading and giving the alarm. Two shots from a gun, for instance, may simply mean that a man has fired the right and left barrel of a shot-gun, but three shots in rapid succession would attract any hunter's or sportsman's attention, and if the three shots were again repeated in the same manner, he would *know* that someone was in trouble.

The author above referred to also states that three stones one on top of the other, three tufts of grass, and three blazes on a tree are signs of danger, but he makes confusion when he puts three smokes for *good* news and *two* smokes for "I am lost, help!" Three of everything does, and should have the same general meaning, a cry for succor, help, and alarm. The white man's custom of three shots as a sign of alarm, the Boy Scouts' custom of three stones, one on top of another, and three blazes on the tree, and three tufts of grass. Three

35

short blasts on a steamboat whistle means full spead astern
that is, to back at full speed! All these things indicate
trouble, consequently in this system of signs I have taken
the liberty of ignoring any apparent exceptions to the rule,
most of which are unimportant or evident mistakes by the
type-setter or stenographer, and I have put down three to
always mean danger.*

It is interesting to note that the hobo signs are full of
warnings and danger from policeman, fierce dogs and surly
householders, while in the hunters' and Indian signs there
are but few devoted to danger, while many are devoted to
objects, such as game, birds, trees, stones, hills, mountains,
rivers, lakes, etc.

It is only the Indians who give us the signs for the weather,
the earth and the sky, and the natural phenomena; by combination, however, of the Indian, the yeggman, and the hobo,
the prospector and the explorer, we have a very complete
system, not only of road, trail and map signs, but ideographs
which may be used in lengthy communications.

SIGNS OF DANGER AND TROUBLE

41 **3** HELP!

Fig. 41. Help.   Numeral "3"
(almost universal sign).*

42 IN TROUBLE!
HELP!

Fig. 42. Indian signs representing three smokes, a warning. When
the Indian makes a signal fire of
dry grass or leaves, he makes the
smoke signal by covering it with a

---

* Sometimes a multiple of the numeral "3" is used. For instance, in
the far North, three shots is sometimes followed by three more in quick
succession to indicate dire distress, and, "The general attention or emergency
call for use on cable or land telegraph lines is the numeral 9." (U. S. Army
Signal Book.)

blanket and then quickly removing the blanket. This causes the smoke to ascend in a balloon-shaped bulb. The sign of alarm with the Apache is three smokes, which signifies danger or the approach of an enemy. (U. S. Eth. Report.)

43 ILL TEMPERED MAN HERE. DANGER!

Fig. 43. A parrallelogram with a dot in the center indicates the presence of danger of some kind, usually means a dangerous man. (Hobo and yeggman sign.) A circle with a dot in the center has the same meaning among the tramps as the rectangle with a dot, but I have omitted it here because Gen. Baden-Powell in his Scout book uses this sign to indicate "I have gone home." These two meanings would tend to confuse our signals. (Egyptian and Chinese sign for sun.)

44 BAD DOG HERE.

Fig. 44. The rectangle with the fence inside of it. There is a dangerous dog in the yard or house. A very useful sign for anyone. (Hobo.)

45 DISHONEST MAN HERE.

Fig. 45. Tells us that a dishonest or unreliable man lives here. In ancient magic it is the sign of Jupiter; among the yeggmen and underworld people, it tells them where they can dispose of stolen goods. With us it indicates people to avoid. (Hobo and yeggmen sign.)

46 THERE ARE THIEVES ABOUT. — Fig. 46. A sign of caution, to let you know that thieves are among you. Keep your eyes on the ten fingers of the pickpockets. (Old English shopkeepers' signs.)

47 $\frac{2}{10}$ WATCH OUT FOR THIEVES. — Fig. 47. 2 on 10, sometimes used verbally, same as Fig. 46. (English tradesmen's sign.)

48 A CRIME HAS BEEN COMMITTED HERE — Fig. 48. Warning. A crime has recently been committed here; it is not a safe place. (Hobo sign.)

49 BE PREPARED TO DEFEND YOUR SELF — Fig. 49. Warning. It may be necessary to defend yourself. (Hobo.)

50 BAD MAN WITH GUN HERE. — Fig. 50. Warning. Look out for gunmen. (Hobo sign.)

51 DESTRUC-TION — Fig. 51. Destruction. Used on map to indicate house or bridge which has been destroyed. (J. B. Tighe.)

52 A BLOW, A KICK AWAITS YOU HERE. — Fig. 52. Warning. Keep away. Avoid this place. Somebody is waiting to beat or punish you. (Hobo sign.)

53 SPOILED — Fig. 53. Inverted pyramid. Marks roads infested by tramps. Hobo sign.)

54 DANGEROUS NEIGHBORHOOD — Fig. 54. Combination of two hobo signs; the sign "here" see Fig. 88 and the sign "danger" Fig. 43. Means dangerous neighborhood here, or danger here. (Hobo or yeggmen.)

55 DISPUTE. BATTLE.

Fig. 55. Discussion, dispute, fight or battle. (Boy Scout sign.)

56 BAD. ENEMY.

Fig. 56. Heart upside down means bad heart, or in other words a bad person. (Boy Pioneer sign.)

57 DOUBTFUL

Fig. 57. With the wilderness scouts, according to Mr. Tighe, (map sign) this represents the earth, but it is only so used in connection with some other sign to represent under or above the earth. As a chalk hobo sign used alone, it stands for the word "doubtful." (Hobo.)

58 NO USE

Fig. 58. A carelessly drawn circle. Nothing doing. If chalked on a fence it tells one that there is no use travelling this way. (Hobo sign.)

CHAPTER V

DANGER, NAUTICAL

BLUE WATER SIGNS OF DANGER AND DISTRESS; SIGNALS BY GUNS; SIGNALS BY ROCKETS; SIGNALS BY EXPLOSIVES; SIGNALS BY SMOKE; SIGNALS BY FOG-HORN; SIGNALS BY BELLS AND WHISTLES

BACK in the days of clipper ships, the Yankee tars had their brawny arms tattooed with pictures in red and blue, representing the Goddess of Liberty and their broad chests adorned with the full-rigged good ship Constitution. In those days all small boys had a romantic desire to go to sea and many a country boy ran away from home for that purpose; among the latter was the writer's own grandfather.

It was in those romantic days of lean, black slave ships with rakish masts and piratical crews, of three-decked, three-masted wooden men of war, with snowy decks and shining brass, that all nautical terms and signs were common knowledge among the readers of fiction both young and old, but now in these modern days of metal boats, towering battleships and murderous submarines many of the old nautical terms, signs and signals can only be found in dusty books on the shelves of second-hand book stores. No longer can a ship "doff its bonnet" as commanded by good King John; no longer does any sailor outside of a newspaper comic page "shiver his timbers"; no longer does the skull and cross bones or the "Jolly Rodger" flying from the masthead of a stranger ship cause the crew of the timid merchantman to throw up their hands in despair. Nevertheless there are still in use many danger signs which not only should be familiar to all seamen but also to all who sail the ocean for pleasure.

Help may be needed or asked for at any time and the nautical sign language should be understood by all.

40

Nautical Distress Signals

When a vessel is in distress and needs assistance from other vessels or from the shore, the following shall be the signals, to be used or displayed by her, either together or separately, namely:

In the daytime:

First—A gun or other explosive signal fired at intervals of about a minute. (U. S. Army Signal Book, 1916.)

Second—The International Code Signal of distress indicated by N. C. (Fig. 182½) U. S. Army Signal Book, 1916.)

Third—The distance signal, consisting of a square flag having either above or below it a ball or anything resembling a ball. (U. S. Army Signal Book, 1916.)

Fourth—A continuous sounding with any fog signal apparatus. (U. S. Army Signal Book, 1916.)

By night:

First—A gun or other explosive signal fired at intervals of about a minute. (U. S. Army Signal Book, 1916.)

Second—Flames on the vessel, as from a burning tar barrel, oil barre land so forth. (U. S. Army Signal Book.)

Third—Rockets or shells throwing stars of any color or description, fired one at a time, at short intervals. (U. S. Army Signal Book, 1916.)

Fourth—A continuous sounding with any fog signal apparatus. (U. S. Army Signal Book, 1916.)

Emergency Signals with Bombs (or Other Explosive), Small Arms, or the National Ensign

A general attention or alarm signal, indicating attack, riot, conflagration, or other emergency, will be made by sound signals, when authorized as previously indicated, by one discharge of a cannon, rifle, pistol or *smoke* bomb by day, followed by a red rocket at half-minute intervals. At night, by one discharge of the cannon, small arm or *light* bomb, followed by a red rocket at half-minute intervals. This signal requires no answer.

Used as an emergency signal it will serve to call attention, and should be followed by a preconcerted signal to indicate the character of the alarm given or to communicate instructions. As an instance, a smoke bomb followed by a rocket is a call to attention and will indicate riot or attack. Should the first rocket be followed by a second, the signal will indicate a flood, a conflagration or other danger.

If no bombs or rockets are at hand at the camp or station for use with sound signals of this character, a general alarm signal will be made by a rapid discharge of shots. None of these signals require an answer. (U. S. Army Signal Book, 1916.)

EMERGENCY SIGNALS BY SOUND WITH BELL, WHISTLE, FOG-HORN, BUGLE, TRUMPET, OR DRUM

General attention, distress or alarm signal may be made by rapidly repeated strokes of the bell, blast of fog-horn or whistle, call of bugle or trumpet, or tap of drum. These signals, explained beforehand and thoroughly understood, require no acknowledgment, but should be acted upon immediately.

In addition to the dot and dash signal, the bugle, the trumpet and the whistle may be used for signaling as in the Drill and Field Service Regulations of the Army (and Boy Scouts).

The long roll of the drum will be recognized as an emergency signal. When used in the Army it is a general-alarm signal and requires all troops to fall into ranks.

During the War of the States the long roll was well understood by everyone; at the sound of the drum the women would gather up their jewels and valuables preparatory to flight and the small boys would—well guess—yes, they would make a break for the trenches in hopes of seeing a battle!

EMERGENCY SIGNALS WITH THE VERY PISTOL

The red star made and repeated with the Very pistol in quick succession as a call, without the rocket, is a signal of distress or alarm, indicating attack, shipwreck, man overboard, fire or other emergency. It must be answered by all stations receiving the signal and requires immediate and proper attention. It is well adapted for use at seacoast stations or on transports.

No preconcerted emergency signals are prescribed for use with visual signals other than pyrotechnics. (U. S. Army Signal Book.)

"It is recommended that the instructions regarding emergency signals, their use and meaning, be posted in all radio and signal stations of the army, at headquarters in garrison or in the field, at the guardhouse of military posts, at the guard tents of troops in the field, and that they be communicated as part of the instructions to officers and to soldiers on guard duty." This should also apply to Boy Scouts, Boy Pioneers, Girl Pioneers, Camp-fire Girls and Girl Scouts, as well as all seaside hotels.

CHAPTER VI

TRAIL SIGNS FOR DANGER, CAUTION, CALAMITY AND CRIES IN THE WILDERNESS FOR HELP

Danger Signs on the Streets and on the Ice. Straw, Grass, Flags, Stones and Sticks as Trouble Signs

On the other side of waters, straw is used very commonly as sign of danger. A bundle of straw hanging from the arch of a bridge tells the traveler that it is undergoing repairs or is in a dangerous condition. Some wisps of straw in a horse's tail is a warning to all people to keep away from its heels because it is a kicker. A handful of straw tied to a stall-post in a stable, barn or hitching post at the fair or tavern warns the public that the horse standing there is a vicious animal and will kick.

Vicious bulls are often labeled by having straw tied to their horns or bunches of straw tied at the top of a pole in the fields where the bulls are grazing or fastened to the gates leading to the pasture. One cannot coax a tramp in South Ireland to enter a gate decorated with a wisp of straw, for that is a notice that ill-tempered dogs are on the premises.

Weak places in the ice, air holes, etc., are strewn with straw as a warning to the skater. Bunches of the straw are used in London to denote danger in the streets where repairing is being done.

Among sportsmen in the Old World, especially in England, straw at the top of a tall red pole warns the fox hunters that there is a barbed wire fence or other danger ahead and during the shooting season the peasantry are warned, by stakes with straw attached, that the "gentry" are shooting there and it is a dangerous ground.

44

Masons in Denmark and Norway and roof-makers in Germany use bundles of straw to warn the passerby of danger overhead; but I know of no instances of straw being used in this manner as a danger signal in this country, unless it is the three tufts of grass Fig. 62. However, it might be appropriate to include a large bunch of grass suspended from a pole or some prominent place as a danger sign, here in America.

 A CALL FOR HELF

Fig. 59. The United States flag is used to designate the condition of the garrison, fort, ship or camp. In times of dire distress, the flag is run part way up the mast or staff with the Union Jack upside down. Whenever this is seen it is an appeal for assistance, telling one that the people in camp, or aboard the ship, are in dire need of help. See Chapter XIV, Fig. 182.

 DANGER HELP!

Fig. 60. Three stones piled one on another; danger or help needed. (Boy Scout sign.)

 DANGER HELP!

Fig. 61. Three sticks driven in the ground. Danger. Help needed. (Boy Scout sign.)

 DANGER HELP!

Fig. 62. Three wisps of grass each with ends tied together. Danger. Help. (Scout sign.)

 HELP!

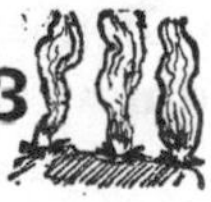

Fig. 63. Three smudge fires burning, enemy approaching. I am lost, in distress, help wanted. (Apache Indian sign.)

Fig. 64. Whenever you hear in the woods three reports of a gun at regular intervals about as you would count 1-2-3, you must give it your immediate attention. In the Northwest, at Mt. McKinley region and Alaska hunting ground, Mr. Belmore Browne tells me they fire the three shots and then three more shots to be sure to attract attention, but in other localities, usually three

64   HELP!

shots are sufficient to call for help, and more is a waste of ammunition which must be conserved under such circumstances

We cannot be too careful in regard to our "trouble" signs, for life often depends upon making them understood; so keep the number 3 in your mind as always meaning danger, trouble or a cry for help and as a sign that should be recognized by all woodsmen.

65    SICKNESS IN CAMP

Fig. 65. A piece of bark or wisp of grass hung on the limb of a tree or on a tripod means that someone is sick in camp. "Smoking a piece of birch-bark and hanging it on a tree means, "I am sick." (J. W. Powell, U. S. Ethnological Report.)

66    HAVE HAD BAD LUCK

Fig. 66. Bark removed near the butt of a tree. Bad luck. (Indian sign.)

67

HAVE MET
CALAMITY

Fig. 67. All the bark removed means a grave and dangerous situation. According to H. L. Masta, Chief of the Abnaki Indians, cutting the bark off from a tree on one, two, three, or four sides near the butt is to be read "have had poor, poorer, poorest luck." Cutting it off all around the tree, "I am starving."

CHAPTER VII

SIGNS OF GOOD LUCK

GOOD FORTUNE, PLENTY, AND JOY

IT is to be expected that there should be a dearth of these signs in the underworld, that is, no signs conveying the meaning of good fortune as we understand it.

For among the outcast, parasites, and degenerates the word good does not convey the same idea as it does to honest folks.

The underworld is essentially selfish, mean, deceitful and treacherous; the criminals band together not thru affection for each other but for mutual protection, like wolves, and such people cannot experience or understand real joy, for they, like the autocratic governments abroad, have their hands raised against every one and everyone's hands are raised against them. Hence there is always a sinister meaning to good luck signs among the yeggmen, tramps and outcast. Good means a good "crib to crack," that is a rich house to rob or a rich man to hold up. There can be no real joy among such people, consequently no sign to represent it.

Nevertheless, we can attach our own meaning to their good luck signs and use them to our advantage, for instance, the letter V is a sign which dead beats, tramps and hoboes understand to mean that people live in the house so marked who are easily imposed upon and can be relied upon to care for a sick beggar or tramp.

But the Scouts can use that sign to designate any hospitable, kind-hearted person upon whom they may depend in time of trouble. In other words, there is nothing wrong with the signs themselves, it is the use that is made of them which makes them good or bad. When we choose to use them, we do so as our parson might say, "for the glory of God."

CHALK-SIGNS FOR GOOD FORTUNE, GOOD LUCK, ETC.

68 ┼   ALL RIGHT. OK.   Fig. 68. A simple cross which is a mark for O.K., all right. (European Hobo sign.) But an X is the automobile sign for a R.R. crossing in America and for cross roads in France. See Chap. 3, Plate 1.

69 \/   IF SICK, WILL CARE FOR YOU;   Fig. 69. A sign shaped like the letter V tells that the people will take care of you if you are sick. (Hobo sign.)

70    KIND GOOD WOMAN   Fig. 70. A rude representation of a cat denotes the house thus decorated to be the home of a kind-hearted woman. (Hobo sign.)

71 SUNSHINE IN THE HEART   Fig. 71. Cheerful, joyous, merry, sunshine in the heart. Generally used as a wish. (Combination Boy Pioneer and Indian sign.)

72 JOYFUL   Fig. 72. Heart song, joyful. (Modified Indian sign.)

73 WEALTH   Fig. 73. Silk hat and a pile of gold, means wealth, plenty. (Yeggmen sign.)

74 PLENTY   Fig. 74. A circle, a forked stick and a buffalo skull, tells us of abundance and plenty. Sometimes the circle or corral has a rude sketch of horse inside. (Indian.)

Fig. 75. Circle with the dash intersecting it. Worth while. On the trail it may indicate that it will be worth while to continue traveling in direction marked; with the underworld it tells the place is worth robbing. (Yeggmen's sign.)

Fig. 76. The Swastika. With the Indians this is probably a modification of the sign of the four winds or the four parts of the earth. (See Fig. 152) now popularly accepted as standing for good luck, used more as a wish than as a statement of the fact. (Ancient religious symbol.)

Fig. 77. A rude indication of a face with two staring eyes, tells the wayfarer that the place so marked is safe camp, a camp where one will not be molested. (Hobo sign.)

CHAPTER VIII

WORD SIGNS

Some Signs not Otherwise Classified, for Convenience Here Called Word-signs

SOME signs represent things, some represent ideas, some signs represent conditions, while others represent time, weather, direction or tell certain secrets, but the following signs are mostly what, for convenience, we will call word signs, and as such are very useful in telling a connected story. For instance, we here have signs for anger, trade, hunger, talk, etc., as well as the famous easy mark most detested by those best entitled to wear it.

Chalk Word-Signs

78 ✕ TRADE

Fig. 78. Trade. A chalk or pencil X is trade, swap, bargain.

79 AFRAID

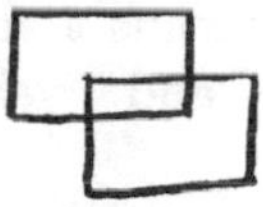

Fig. 79. Is afraid, timid, nervous, cowardly. (Hobo.)

80 ANGER

Fig. 80. Anger. Thunder in the heart. (Combination of Indian and Scout signs.)

81 HUNGER

Fig. 81. Hunger. Supposed to be a man with a black dash across his stomach which tells of hunger. (Many Indian tribes.)

82  EASY

Fig. 82. Easymark. Indicates an easy trail, but with hoboes and tramps it indicates a person who is easily buncoed; it is the letter "Teth" in writing called "Passing the River" and the letter Gimel in the celestial writing claimed to be "the mysterious character of letters delivered by Honorious, called Theban alphabet of the ancient magic." (Probably borrowed from the gypsies by the tramps.)

83 TALK

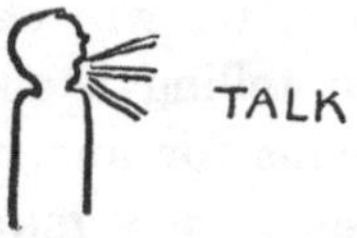

Fig. 83. Talk. Rude figure of man with double lines issuing from mouth; it tells of a talk or of talking. Among the Dakotas, whooping-cough is represented with a single line issuing from the mouth. (Indian sign.)

84 SHOUT

Fig. 84. Shout. Rude figure of a man with three heavy lines issuing from mouth means a shout, shouting, hallooing and yelling. (Indian sign.)

85 SONG

Fig. 85. Song. Wavy lines issuing from mouth means a song, singing or melody. (Indian signs.)

86 IN

Fig. 86. In. A letter C turned backwards when marked on the door means that the owner is in. (Hobo.) From the letter Caph in the magic writing called Malachim.

87 OUT

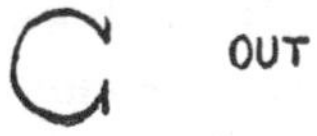

Fig. 87. Out. The same letter reversed means that the occupant of the house, tent, or camp is out.

(Hobo.) Although this looks like the letter C, it is in reality the letter "Caph" from the Ancient magic. (Hobo.)

88 □ HERE

Fig. 88. Here. This is the place. Here. This is a new but useful tramp sign, it was furnished to the writer by Hon. Geo. Porter, Director of Public Safety of Philadelphia. (Tramp sign.)

CHAPTER IX

MAP SIGNS OF PEOPLE

Signs for Maps and Fences Telling of Men, Women, and Children. White, Yellow, Red and Black Men, Officers and Doctors, Scouts and "Justicers"

It is often necessary and useful to inform our friends, our clan, our Scouts, our fellow explorers, just what sort of people we have met; just what people they will meet on the trail. The Knights of the Road have found this to be particularly useful to them and hence the fences are often decorated with many queer chalk-signs, unintelligible to the respectable citizen, but when seen by the yeggman or the hobo, he immediately understands them and knows what sort of a person is to be found in the houses decorated with these chalk-signs. For this purpose there are signs to represent magistrates, policemen, etc.

But these signs, like all of the others, are taken from the underworld and may be used to advantage by honest people, and are particularly useful to mapmakers, hunters, travelers, Scouts and soldiers.

Chalk- and Map-Signs Indicating People

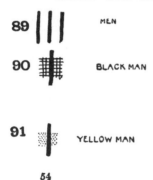

89 — MEN

Fig. 89. Men. Upright marks indicating men. (Map signs, Tighe.)

90 — BLACK MAN

Fig. 90. Negro. Heraldic sign for black over upright line for man indicates a negro. (Combination map and Heraldry.)

91 — YELLOW MAN

Fig. 91. Chinaman. Heraldic sign for yellow combines with the sign for man meaning a Chinaman

54

or Japanese. (Combination map and Heraldry.)

92 〔sign〕   RED MAN

Fig. 92. Indian. Heraldic sign for red with a map sign for man meaning an Indian. (Combination map and Heraldry.)

93 〔sign〕   GENTLEMAN

Fig. 93. Gentlemen. Rude drawing of a tall hat with the hoboes means rich man, with the Indians white man, but with the reader it means a gentleman. (Hobo sign.)

94 〔sign〕   OFFICER SCOUT MASTER

Fig. 94. Scoutmaster. Sign for an officer of any kind, but as we have two other signs for officer, it is thought wise to limit this to Scoutmaster or leader. (Hobo.)

95 〔sign〕   JUDGE

Fig. 95. Judge. Means a judge or a magistrate used by tramps to indicate any sort of an officer of the law. (Tramp sign.)

96 〔sign〕   POLICEMAN

Fig. 96. Policeman. A sword means a policeman; this is a European sign and it is the sword of the Gendarmes. (Foreign tramp sign.)

97 〔sign〕   DOCTOR

Fig. 97. Doctor. Skull and cross-bones, a doctor. (Yegg. sign.)

98 〔sign〕   SCOUTS

Fig. 98. Scout. Powder-horn means scouts. (Boy Pioneer sign.)

99 〔sign〕   WOMAN

Fig. 99. A woman. (Hobo.)

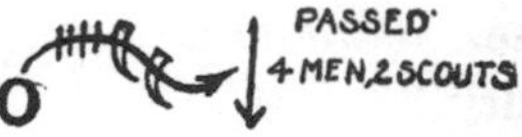

Fig. 100. This, combined with the arrow pointing down, means something that has happened; the four straight lines indicating men, the two powder-horns, Scouts; the arrow points on wavy lines show direction, means four men and two scouts passed this way. (Foreign hobo sign.)

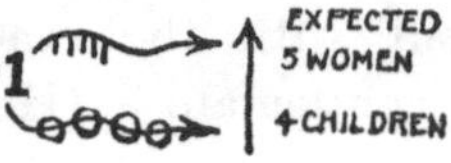

Fig. 101. With the tramps, in this instance, a woman is only half a man, consequently the half lines represent women and for some reason they use their sign of "nothing doing" to represent children, these two combined with the arrow pointing upward means something which *is to come*, and would read "five women and four children *will* pass this way, this would usually be expressed with women and children on the one arrow shaft. (Hobo sign.)

CHAPTER X

CHALK- AND MAP-SIGNS OF ANIMALS

THE conventional signs used in map-making are familiar to most people, but there are some signs with which few are acquainted, for instance, on insurance maps there are conventional signs to represent the sort of roof, the height of fire walls and the material of which the buildings are constructed. Thus a diagram of a house colored yellow is known to represent a frame building, but if it is colored red it is a brick house and if colored blue it is a stone building.

So also if it has a black dot on it the insurance people know that the building has a tar and gravel roof. If it has a small cross on it that tells us that the house has a shingle roof, while a little circle indicates a metal or slate roof. But for ordinary field work we do not need these signs for there may be no building on our map but it behooves the explorer, scout, hunter, or aviator to note the presence of horses and cattle or of wild game animals all of which are important to the explorer and Scout, while to the army, horses may indicate the presence of cavalry.

These signs are particularly interesting to hunters of big game, for with them, on a rough map, they can designate the point where they have seen sheep, goat, elk, or deer; also they are useful to rangers to show on a map where the cattle and horses are grazing and whether the same belong to them or not. These signs are also particularly interesting to the young people to be used in their picturegraph writing.

57

CHALK- AND MAP-SIGNS TO DESIGNATE DOMESTIC OR WILD ANIMALS

102 ⋀⋀⋀ DOG

Fig. 102. Composed of two letter W's joined together. Sometimes used by the tramps to designate a dog. Why this form of sign is used is unknown, unless it be to represent the motion of a dog as he jumps up and down while barking at a stranger. (Hobo.)

103 PIG

Fig. 103. Pig. (Children's sign.)

104 ♉ ♉ CATTLE

Fig. 104. Horned cattle, may mean elk, deer, antelope or domestic cattle; on a hunter's map it would probably mean elk or deer. (Map sign.)

105 HERD OF CATTLE

Fig. 105. The same sign with three at the bottom and one or two over it indicates a herd of horned beasts, multitudes of them, many of them. (Map sign.)

106 OUR CATTLE

Fig. 106. The same sign with a curved line over it would mean *our* herd of cattle. (Map sign.)

107 V V SHEEP

Fig. 107. A couple of V's stand for sheep, these last four signs are used on hunters' and explorers' maps. (Tighe, Outdoor Life.)

108   GOATS   Fig. 108. Goats. In the wilderness, these would mean Rocky Mountain goats, or wild goats of some kind. (Map signs.)

109   HORSES   Fig. 109. Horses. (Map signs, Tighe.)

110   A HORSEMAN   Fig. 110. Horseman. (Map signs, Tighe.)

CHAPTER XI

SIGNS OF INANIMATE OR MOTIONLESS THINGS

MAP SIGNS, PICTUREGRAPH SIGNS, AND CONVENTIONAL SIGNS

THE conventional signs used on maps, such as the ones indicating mountains, rivers, railroads, lakes, etc., are so well understood by even little children that they can claim no place here.

But there are map signs which are most convenient and particularly valuable to explorers, Scouts and cross country hikers, which are unknown to the majority of people and never seen in the conventional books on map-making.

As a matter of course most of these signs represent inanimate objects, because animated creatures seldom remain in one place long enough to be put on the map except in a general way telling that such and such aminals frequent particular spots; but a spring, a well and a house properly belong on topographical maps, that is on maps of land as viewed from an aëroplane.

The following signs are particularly useful to surveyors, army officers, explorers and hunters when making rough maps of the country, as by these signs they can designate where their food is cached, that is hidden away, where there is fodder for their animals, the location of stone cairns and so forth, and any signs that are useful to the above mentioned people are especially useful to the Boy Scouts and even Girl Pioneers, Girl Scouts and Camp-fire Girls.

CHALK- AND MAP-SIGNS OF INANIMATE THINGS

111 FOOD FOR MAN Fig. 111. Crude drawing of a mouth. Means food for man. (Map sign.)

112 FOOD FOR HORSES Fig. 112. Rude outline of a haystack, means food for horses and cattle. (Map sign, Tighe.)

113 CAIRN Fig. 113. Three stones with two stones on them means a stone-pile or cairn, usually used to mark a corner of a tract of land, or a spot where something is cached or hidden. (Map and Mexican sign combined.)

114 —— O ROUND Fig. 114. A straight line is used to represent the ground when in connection with some other sign. See Fig. 115. (Map sign.)

115 CACHED FOOD) Fig. 115. Illustrates the use of Fig. 114, in this instance it represents buried food, food under-ground. (Map sign.) With the outline of a pyramid under it, it will designate buried treasures or gold.

116 HILL Fig. 116. Contour lines repre-senting a hill, mountain or eleva-tion of some kind. (Surveyor's sign.)

117 TELEPHONE Fig. 117. A rude drawing of a bird means a telephone. (Hobo sign.)

118 RAILROAD Fig. 118. A rude drawing of an engine, means railroad. (Hobo sign.)

119 TROLLEY Fig. 119. A rude drawing of a trolley-car, means trolley. (Hobo sign.)

120   HOSPITAL   Fig. 120. A Red Cross flag, means a hospital. (Boy Scout sign.)

121   DRUG-STORE   Fig. 121. Rough sketch of a mortar and pestle stands for a drug store. (Boy Pioneers.)

122   JAIL   Fig. 122. Cross bars, stands for a jail. (Yegg. sign.)

123   CHURCH   Fig. 123. Cross in a circle stands for a church. (Boy Pioneer sign.) A circle around any object stands for a corral or a house, thus a circle around a policeman may read, a police station.

124   COURT HOUSE   Fig. 124. A rough spiral in a circle, literally an enclosed magistrate stands for a court house. (Combined signs.)

125   FIRE ENGINE HOUSE   Fig. 125. Fire engine house. (Tramp and Indian sign combined.)

126   HOUSE   Fig. 126. A house. (Military map sign.)

127   TENTS   Fig. 127. Tents. (Map sign; also Indian sign for tepee.)

128   BRIDGE   Fig. 128. Bridge. (Civil engineer sign.)

129   BOAT   Fig. 129. Boat. (Map sign.)

130   SAIL BOAT   Fig. 130. A sail boat. (Map sign.)

131   SHIP OR SCHOONER   Fig. 131. A ship or schooner. (Map sign.)

132   STEAMBOAT   Fig. 132. A steamboat. (Map sign.)

132½   SUBMARINE   Fig. 132½. Submarine. (Map sign.)

133   A TREE   Fig. 133. A tree, rude form of a tree, with a shadow. (Map sign.)

134   A FOREST   Fig. 134. Three trees with two over them, sign of a forest. (Map sign.)

135   A STONE   Fig. 135. A stone. (Aztec sign.)

Although trees and vegetation have life and are therefore not inanimate objects, they are motionless and it has been found convenient to place them on this list where they more properly belong then they do among the animals.

CHAPTER XII

SIGNS OF THE ELEMENTS

Map or Picturegraph Signs of Fire, Air, Water, Earth, Wind, Rainbow, Sea, Lake and Ocean, Thunder, Lightning and the Four Winds of the Earth

These signs include fire, air, and water, and like celestial signs, they are mostly borrowed from the Red men. Hoboes and yeggmen take little interest in celestial objects, and unlike the proverbial Kentucky Colonel, they do not even use water for bathing purposes. But in the wilderness life itself often depends upon the traveler's ability to find water, and among the ordinary pedestrians, Boy Scouts and Girl Pioneers, Camp-fire Girls, and Girl Scouts, it is absolutely necessary for the hikers and Scoutmasters to be able to direct the followers to the location of good water which is uncontaminated by the dreaded typhoid germs.

Signs of the Elements

Map, Chalk- or Picture-Writing Signs

Fig. 136. Smoke. Indian sign, supposed to be the balloon-shaped puff of smoke arising from the smudge fire, from which a blanket has suddenly been removed.

Fig. 137. Fire. (Combination sign.)

Fig. 138. Fresh water. This is a map sign. Hoboes use the same sign to represent a poor man, probably meaning a man who

is too poor to drink anything but water, but the poverty meaning of the sign may best be forgotten and thus prevent confusion.

139 UNDERGROUND WATER. A SPRING.

Fig. 139. A spring. Sign of ground over the sign of fresh water is the sign of underground water or a well. (Map sign, Tighe.)

140 GOOD DRINKING WATER

Fig. 140. Good drinking water. Sign of good heart and the sign of water combined. (Map and Scout signs.)

141 BAD DRINKING WATER

Fig. 141. Bad drinking water. (Map and Scout signs.)

142 DANGEROUS DRINKING WATER

Fig. 142. Dangerous drinking water. (Hobo and Map sign combined.)

143 SHALLOW WATER A FORD

Fig. 143. A ford. Upright lines representing men, the wavy line water, the combination shows that men can wade the water. (Map sign.)

144 LARGE LAKE SEA OR OCEAN

Fig. 144. Large body of water. Sea, lake, or ocean. (Girl Pioneer sign.)

145 RAINBOW

Fig. 145. Rainbow. (Indian sign.)

146 MIST OR CLOUDS

Fig. 146. Cloud, or fog. (Indian sign.)

147 RAIN

Fig. 147. Rain. (Indian sign.)

148 SNOW

Fig. 148. Snow. (Indian sign.)

149 LIGHTNING

Fig. 149. Lightning. (Indian sign)

150 THUNDER

Fig. 150. Thunder. (The thunder bird of the Indians)

151 AIR, WIND

Fig. 151. Air or wind, probably a puff adder. (Indian sign.)

152 THE FOUR WINDS

Fig. 152. The Four Winds, or four parts of the earth. (Indian sign.)

153 WHIRL WIND, TORNADO

Fig. 153. A tornado or whirlwind. (Indian sign.)

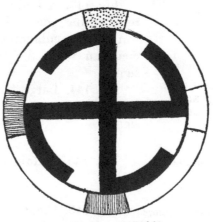

COMPASS INDIAN

CHAPTER XIII

CELESTIAL SIGNS

Sun, Moon, Stars, Constellations and Milky Way

THE modern Indian educated by the whites, as a rule, knows as little of the significance and origin of the conventional signs and ornament in the bead work done by the squaws as do the squaws themselves or the children who buy the trinkets at the curio stores. But the old Indians uncontaminated by the whites, could read the ornaments in the bead and basket work as readily as a modern stenographer can read her own notes after the latter have become "cold" so to speak.

Since the sun represented a day and the moon represented a month these signs frequently appear in Indian ornaments. The sign for the Morning Star is sometimes used for the sign of "Medicine." Medicine, by the way, being a white man's term for what the Indians might more probably translate as "Mystery."

It is unnecessary to say that none of these signs are derived from the hoboes, yeggmen or the underworld, who have little to do with celestial things. But it is interesting to note that they are all signs used by our American Indians. This goes to show that the red savages occupied a higher position in intellectual and moral life than does certain classes of white men. All Sunday School scholars know that St. Luke said "A good man out of the good treasure of his heart bringeth forth that which is good, and an evil man out of the evil treasure of his heart bringeth forth that which is evil." Of course it is taken for granted that all sportsmen are good Sunday School scholars. At any rate we know that all sportsmen are interested in celestial things.

CELESTIAL SIGNS USED IN BASKET WORK, BEAD WORK, NEEDLE WORK, PICTURE-WRITING

154  SUN

Fig. 154. The sun. This may or may not have rays surrounding it or may have a dot in the center. (Indian sign.)

155. MOON

Fig. 155. The moon. A crescent enclosed in a circle to distinguish it from the crescent used to represent a month. (Indian sign.

156. STAR

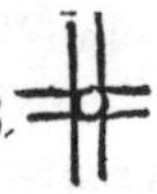

Fig. 156. A star. (Indian sign.)

157 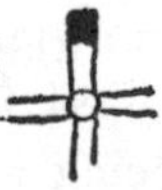 NORTH STAR

Fig. 157. The North star. (Indian sign. Combination.)

158  STAR GROUP

Fig. 158. A star group or a constellation, from a string of beads. (Indian Sign.)

159  MILKY WAY

Fig. 159. The Milky Way. (Indian sign.)

CHAPTER XIV

SIGNS OF COLOR

USED IN HERALDRY, BY WEATHER BUREAU, BY AMERICAN INDIANS IN
SYMBOLISM, AND WITH FLAGS

FOR convenience in printing without colors, certain signs which can be reproduced in black and white have been adopted in heraldry, as for instance, the vertical lines on a field represent red; dots represent yellow, etc. These arbitrary symbols furnish us a means of designating color without using the color itself.

Colors have, in themselves, well-recognized meanings. For instance, red always stands for something doing, for agitation, for life while white has been from time immemorial the sign of peace. Back in 1066 or 1000, according to the Saga of Thorfinn, a lot of natives (possibly Esquimaux) approached the Vikings shaking reeds towards the sun, "then," said Thorfinn "what do you think this means?" Snorri Thorbrandson answered, "Perhaps it is a sign of peace, let us take a WHITE shield and hold it out towards them." The interesting part of this story is that the Vikings used white as a sign of peace and the Esquimaux, or Northern Indians, seemed to recognize the symbol and accepted it with its present meaning, thus white has a well recognized meaning in symbolism. Emanuel Swedenborg is the best authority on symbolism and some of the meanings given by him of the colors are introduced below.

White meaning peace, it was very natural that the weather bureau should use, as it does, a white flag to tell us of clear and fair weather. A blue flag with the weather bureau means rain or snow and so on, while a black triangular flag is known as the temperature signal. When such a flag is placed above the blue flag, it tells the people they may expect warmer weather, when placed below the blue flag it tells the people to expect cold weather. When omitted, one may look for a stationary temperature. A red flag with a black center is a storm signal, but a red pennant without the black center informs us that there is a storm in the vicinity but not one of dangerous proportions. At night, a red light is used for easterly winds and a white and red light for westerly winds. The railroads also have a system of signals of colored flags and colored lights, for instance, red means stop, or danger; it is a color to heed.

Fixing a Standard for American Flags

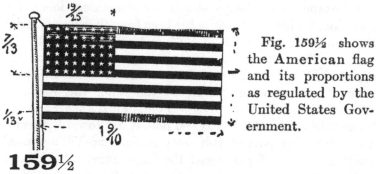

Fig. 159½ shows the American flag and its proportions as regulated by the United States Government.

159½

Because flags have been manufactured with various proportions and with no standard dimensions for the various government departments, the President issued an order giving the requirements of the proportions for "Old Glory."

The President's order prescribes that all national flags and Union Jacks manufactured for the government departments, with the exception of the colors carried by troops, and camp colors, which are provided for in the regulations of the army and navy, shall conform to the following proportions: Hoist (width) of flag 1; fly (length) of flag, 1.9;

hoist (width) of union, $\frac{7}{13}$; fly (length) of union, .76, or $\frac{18}{25}$; width of each stripe, $\frac{1}{13}$

The order further provides the sizes of flags manufactured or purchased for the government departments shall be limited to those with the following hoists:

No. 1, 20 ft.; 2, 19 ft. (standard); 3, 14.35 ft.; 4, 12.19 ft.; 5, 10 ft.; 6, 8.94 ft.; 7, 5.14 ft.; 8, 5 ft.; 9, 3.52 ft.; 10, 2.90 ft.; 11, 2.37 ft.; 12, 1.31 ft.

When in the manufacture of any flag under these specifications the resulting dimensions appear as fractions of an inch, such fractions shall be taken as the nearer inch. In the event of a fraction of exactly a half inch, the whole inch greater shall be adopted.

The order provides that all national flags having hoists less than 5 ft., except colors carried by troops, and the corresponding Union Jack, shall have only 13 stars in the union, in order that the identity of the stars may be plainly distinguishable. The size of the Union Jack shall be the size of the union of the national flag with which it is flown.

The position and size of each star for the unions of 48 and 13 stars, respectively, are also provided. In the case of the national flag, which now has 48 stars, the order provides that they shall be arranged in six rows of eight stars each, with the corresponding stars in each row in a vertical line. The size of the stars in this type of flag is not determined by means of proportion but by a scale prepared by the Navy Department and supplied to the other executive departments. It prescribes that the diameter of a circle, the circumference of which will intersect the five points of the star shall be 1.17 ft. in the case of the flag of type No. 2; .92 ft. in the case of flag No. 3; .83 ft. in the case of flag No. 4; .67 ft. in the case of flag No. 6; .42 ft. in the case of flag No .7, etc.

All flags used by the government are now being made

to conform to the new regulations, and other manufacturers
are adopting the same rule.

160 WHITE, COLOR
CLEAR OR FAIR.
EAST.
TRUTH.

Fig. 160. White.   Clear, or fair
weather.   In symbolism it stands
for purity and truth.   With the
Zuni white is East from whence
the light comes.

161 RED, COLOR
SOUTH
REVOLUTION.
LIFE, AUCTION
LOVE.

Fig. 161. Red.   With the railroads means Stop.   Red is used
in times of . revolution; the red
flag is a sign of danger, of an auction or forced sale.   With the Indians, red means life; it stands
for the life's blood; in symbolism
it is the masculine color and also
stands for love.   With the Zuni,
red represents the South.

162 BLUE · COLOR.
RAIN OR SNOW.
WEST

Fig. 162. Blue.   With rail roads
this means workmen are under the
car.   Weather bureau, rain or snow.
With the Zuni, blue is West.

163 YELLOW·COLOR.
CONTAGIOS DESEASE
NORTH, THE SUN.

Fig. 163. Yellow.   With   the
railroad, yellow means Safe.   A
yellow flag warns you of contagious
diseases.   A yellow ribbon is used
for a chump, or boob mark, by the
Boy Scouts.   The sign of the sun.
Also, the color of the suffragist.
With the Zuni, yellow is North.

164 PURPLE·COLOR
ROYAL.
LOVE OF TRUTH.

Fig. 164. Purple.   A color of
royalty, mourning.   In symbolism
stands for the love of truth.

165 GREEN·COLOR. THE EARTH KNOWLEDGE.

Fig. 165. Green. With the railroad green stands for Caution and green and white means, "flag station." With some Indians green indicates earth, in symbolism it stands for knowledge.

166 BLACK·COLOR. WAR, DEATH, NIGHT. UNDERWORLD FALSEHOOD.

Fig. 166. Black. Night, death, war. In symbolism it is falsehood. With the Zuni, black is the underground world, but many various colors are the signs of the heavens, the overworld, rainbow.

FLAG SIGNS

167 COLD WAVE.

Fig. 167. A cold wave; note that the color symbols are used here to designate the colors of the flags. (Weather bureau and Heraldry.)

168 LOCAL RAINS.

Fig. 168. Local rains. (Weather bureau.)

169 TEMPERATURE

Fig. 169. Temperature Flag. (Weather bureau.) Used alone means stationary weather.

170 STORM

Fig. 170. Storm. (Weather bureau.)

171 EASTERLY STORM NEAR

Fig. 171. A storm near at hand. (Weather bureau.)

172 N.W. WINDS

Fig. 172. Northwest winds. (Weather bureau.) A white pennant alone indicates westerly winds, this is from N. W. to S. W. inclusive, and that the storm center has passed.

173 WARMER

174 WARMER

175 NORTH EASTERLY WINDS

176 COLDER

177 COLDER

178 HURICANE

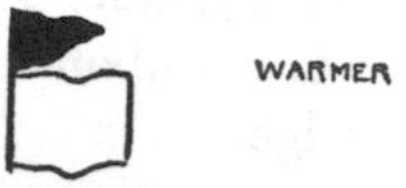

Fig. 173. Warmer weather coming. (Weather bureau.)

Fig. 174. Warmer. The black pennant above the white or blue flag tells us that warmer weather is coming. (Weather bureau.)

Fig. 175. Easterly winds. The red pennant flying above the storm signal tells us that winds are expected from the Northeast. If below the storm signal, it would tell us that the winds were from the Southeast.

Fig. 176. Colder weather coming. (Weather bureau.)

Fig. 177. Colder weather coming. When the black pennant is hoisted below either the white or blue pennant, it indicates a drop of the mercury in the thermometer. (Weather bureau.)

Fig. 178. The red storm flag with the black center; the two flying together tell us of the approach of a hurricane. (Weather bureau.)

VICTORY

EVERY THING SERENE

SOME ONE IS DEAD

A CALL FOR HELP

DISTRESS

PILOT

BLUE PETER

CHOLERA

GUN POWDER

Fig. 179. Two National flags one above the other tell of victory of the top flag and defeat for the bottom one. (Common custom.)

Fig. 180. Flag flying in the breeze at top of staff, all is well.

Fig. 181. Flag at half staff (on shore), half mast (at sea) tells of death, a ship with a flag at half mast tells those on shore that someone has died aboard the ship. (Common usage.)

Fig. 182. Flag upside down is a sign of distress and a call for help. (Common nautical sign.)

Fig. 182½. Signal flags N. C. International Code Signal of distress. (Signal book of United States Army.)

Fig. 182⅓. Pilot signal, a call for a pilot. "I want a pilot."

Fig. 182¼. "Blue Peter," flown by a ship when it is just about to sail.

Fig. 182⅕. The Cholera, yellow fever, or plague flag. Ships flying it are given a wide berth.

Fig. 182⅙. The Powder Flag. It is a red swallow-tailed flag, and is used to warn all persons that the ships flying it are loading or unloading gun-powder.

Fig. 182½. "Jolly Rodjer." The jolly rodjer or black flag became infamous during the era when pirates infested the seas. This flag was also used on the Mexican border in the early days by irregular Mexican troops. The meaning of it is, ' 'no quarter asked or given," that is, no prisoners will be taken, everybody caught will be killed. The skull is still used by the Germans as a decoration for their military hats, and at the present writing they are acting in accord with their gruesome emblem, which they live up to in even a more brutal degree than did the old pirates.

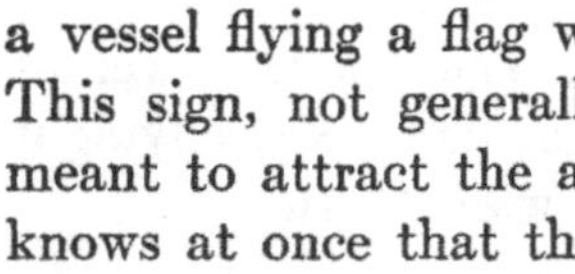

Fig. 183. Custom House officer wanted (nautical), Scoutmaster wanted. (Boy Scout.)

Strangers at any of the big seaports frequently observe a vessel flying a flag with a knot tied in one corner of it. This sign, not generally understood by the landlubber, is meant to attract the attention of the customs officer, who knows at once that the vessel displaying it wishes to ship or to consume a quantity of bonded goods, *i. e.*, tobacco, liquors, etc., his presence being necessary to break the seal before such goods can be utilized.

CHAPTER XV

THERE is a certain charm about the Indian symbols which is lacking in all others; at least so it seems to all real Americans. For the Indian symbols to us are doubly symbolic; they are the signs for the things which the Indians intended to represent and also a register revealing the working of the brains and the hearts of the Indians themselves. These signs bring back to our mind all the poetry, all the vigorous red-blooded adventure, all the dark tragedy and all the mystery of the old frontier life.

Although the symbols painted by the ancient redmen on the weather beaten cliffs still retain their original colors and are capable of being deciphered, or partially so, by experts, they seem to speak to us in grunts like the old Indians themselves, with disjointed words, softened and mellowed by time. They speak with a voice like that recorded for the phonograph of someone long since dead, and it is indeed a voice from the grave of a race in a tongue now half forgotten and seldom understood by even the remnants of their own people.

The hoboes, yeggmen, and gypsies seem to be without symbols representing time, but the American Indians, the ancient magicians, and the Boy Pioneers and Scouts supply us with a very complete system from which we have borrowed and which will be found very useful in cipher communication, price marking on goods for merchants, chalk-signs, picture-writing and for hunters, trappers, explorers

and military men. For instance, if your nickname among
your fellows is "Spades" you make a picture of the ace of
spades, put an arrow with a point down, an arc with a short
line at the center which will read "Spades left here at noon."
As may be seen by the following symbols, Spades could give
the exact day, year and month on which he left that spot

THE BUCKSKIN CALENDAR

	TENDERFEET		2ND CLASS SCOUTS	FIRST CLASS SCOUTS			
	ALMANAC		INDIAN	PIONEER	INVENTED & DESIGNED BY Dan Beard 1911		
NO.	MONTHS	SIGNS	(MOONS)	☾ MOONS ☽		SEASONS	SIGNS
1	JAN- UARY		DIFFICULTY	PIKE 5TH 1779		COTONK	
2	FEB- RUARY		RACCOON	LINCOLN 12TH 1809 WASHINGTON 22ND			
3	MARCH		SORE-EYE	JOHNNY APPLESEED ARBOR DAY		BUDDING	
4	APRIL		GOOSE-EGG	KENTON 3RD 1755			
5	MAY		PLANTING	AUDUBON 4TH 1780		BLOSSOM	
6	JUNE		STRAWBERRY	MARQUETTE 1ST 1637			
7	JULY		BUFFALO	CATLIN 26TH 1796		ROASTING- EAR	
8	AUGUST		HARVEST	CROCKETT 17TH 1786			
9	SEP- TEMBER		WILDRICE	ANDREW FOE 30TH 1742		INDIAN SUMMER	
10	OC- TOBER		NUTS	PENN 14TH 1644			
11	NOV- EMBER		DEER	BOONE 2ND 1734		LEAF-FALLING	
12	DE- CEMBER		WOLVES	CARSON 24TH 1809			

and do this without a letter or a written word, or a numeral recognizable by anyone but the initiated.

The backwoodsmen borrowed their seasons from the Indians, and as late as the writer's own boyhood in Kentucky, the people spoke of the Roasting Ear Season, the Budding Season, and we all still speak of the Indian Summer.

"For the great Michabo sits mid falling leaves
And drowsing, lights the peace pipe of the world;
And as he sits and smokes, a dreamy haze
Spreads thru the land and lingering summer stays."

Of course these seasons over-lap each other, but arbitrarily dividing them into six regular divisions, January and February are winter months and taking them in order they will be read as follows:

January and February........Wild Goose or Winter Season.
March and April.............Budding Season.
May and June................Blossom Season.
July and August.............Roasting Ear Season.
September and October.......Indian Summer.
November and December.....Leaf Falling Season.

SIGNS FOR THE INDIAN SEASONS

The Indians' Moons naturally vary in the different parts of the country, but by comparing them all and striking an average as near as may be, the moons are reduced to the following:

January......Moon of Difficulties, Black Smoke Moon.
February.....Moon of Raccoons, Bare Spots on the Ground Moon.
March........Moon of Winds, Little Grass, Sore Eyes Moon
April.........Moon of Ducks and Goose Eggs.
May.........Moon of Green Grass, Root Food Moon.

June.........Moon of Corn Planting, Strawberry Moon.
July..........Moon of Buffalo (Bull), Hot Sun Moon.
August.......Moon of Harvest, Cow Buffalo Moon.
September....Moon of Wild Rice, Red Plum Moon.
October.......Moon of Leaf Falling, Nuts Moon.
November....Moon of Deer Mating, Fur Pelts Moon.
December.....Moon of Wolves, Big Moon.

The signs representing time were first collected for the use of the Boy Scouts of the Sons of Daniel Boone or Boy Pioneers.

Signs of Time

184 PAST, GONE — Fig. 184. Arrow pointing down. Past or gone. (Boy Pioneer sign.)

185 PRESENT-NOW — Fig. 185. Arrow pointing both ways. To-day, now, present time. (Boy Pioneer sign.)

186 FUTURE TO COME — Fig. 186. Arrow pointing up. Time to come, future, to-morrow, next week. (Boy Pioneer sign.)

187 DAY — Fig. 187. Sign for day. (Various Indian tribe's sign.)

188 SUNRISE — Fig. 188. Sunrise. (Ojibway Indians.)

189 FORENOON — Fig 189. Forenoon. (Ojibway Indians.)

190 NOON — Fig. 190. Noon. (Ojibway Indians.)

190½ AFTERNOON — Fig. 190½. Afternoon. (Ojibway Indians.)

191 NIGHT — Fig. 191. Night. (Ojibway Indians.)

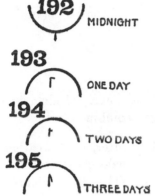

192 MIDNIGHT

Fig. 192.   Midnight.

193 ONE DAY

Fig. 193. One day. (Indian and ancient magic combined.)

194 TWO DAYS

Fig. 194.   Two days.   (Indian and ancient magic combined.)

195 THREE DAYS

Fig. 195.   Three days. (Indian and ancient magic combined.)

196 FOUR DAYS.

Fig. 196.   Four days.   (Indian and ancient magic.)

197 FIVE DAYS

Fig. 197.   Five days.   (Indian and ancient magic.)

198 SIX DAYS

Fig. 198.   Six days.   (Indian and ancient magic.)

199 WEEK

Fig. 199.   Seven days or week. (Indian and ancient magic.)

200 TWO WEEKS

Fig. 200.   Two weeks.   (Indian and ancient magic.)

201 THREE WEEKS

Fig. 201.   Three weeks.   (Indian and ancient magic.)

Fig. 202. A Month. (Indian sign.)

Fig. 203. A Year. (Indian and ancient magic combined.)

Fig. 204. Winter, cold weather, the Cohonk or wild goose season of the Indians. The first diagram shows the simplified form of drawing the goose (Boy Pioneer sign)

Fig. 205. Spring. The Budding season of the Indians; first diagram shows simplified form of drawing buds. (Pioneer sign.)

Fig. 206. Summer. The Roasting Ear Season of the Indians. (Pioneer sign.)

Fig. 207. Fall. The Leaf Falling Season of the Indians. (Pioneer signs.)

CHAPTER XVI

SECRET WRITING—THE CABALA

Use in Ancient Magic and by the Children of To-day; Secret Cost Marks used by Merchants

Besides the Cabalistic letters and figures the tit-tat-toe system, there is given on Fig. 207A an alphabet of musical notes, which can be used as a written alphabet disguised by putting the notes on bars of music, or may be sounded on musical instruments, as the cornet or bugle.

BUGLE NUMERALS

This musical alphabet was sent to the writer by Mr. Thomas McHugh, of Jamaica Plains, Mass. He explains that in giving the call on the bugle the bugler is to tongue every note good and strong, to pause at the end of each word, and end each message with a high note.

It will be interesting to the boys to use this alphabet in written messages, which was not thought of by its inventor. For instance, you make what is apparently a bar of music, like that at the bottom of Fig. 207A, but which really is a hidden message that reads, "Boy Scouts." Messages of any length may be thus written that might easily escape the notice of even suspicious persons, and hence be of use not only to Boy Scouts but to our Secret Service, and if we can be of any service to Uncle Sam we will be indeed happy.

SECRET OR CIPHER WRITING

In the books of ancient magic almost all of the hobo signs of to-day will be found, also the ancient "Cabala," which is nothing more than our modern tit-tat-toe sign. (Fig. 207A.) But in the ancient magic the Cabala was considered a sacred emblem and by tables made from it the old magicians and astrologers made "Calculations of the names of spirits good and bad and under the presidency of the seven planets and twelve militant signs" whatever that means. The secret alphabet, however, has been known to schoolboys for ages. For instance, the first division in the left-hand corner we call "A." Make an upright line across the bottom of this division and it is "B," put a cap to upright line and it is "C." Then the next division is "D,E,F"; and so it goes on through the mystic courts or divisions of the figure.

In Trinity Church Yard in New York City, one of the old grave stones has an epitaph written in the sign letters of the Cabala. But if I remember aright, in this case, in place of using dashes they use dots and in place of beginning at the upper left-hand corner they began somewhere on the opposite side.

Thus they would use one division or "court" for "A" as we have done in the table, then the same court with a dot for "B" and again with two dots for "C." But the simplest and most direct method is shown here, which the reader may vary to any extent he chooses so as to mystify his friends or the public.

The tit-tat-toe system of numerals here shown for the first time is entirely new and possesses the advantage of being susceptible of combinations up to four figures which suggests nothing to the uninitiated but a sort of Japanese form of decoration. For instance, (Figure 207B) the numeral "one" is the reversed " ⌐ "-shaped first division, ten

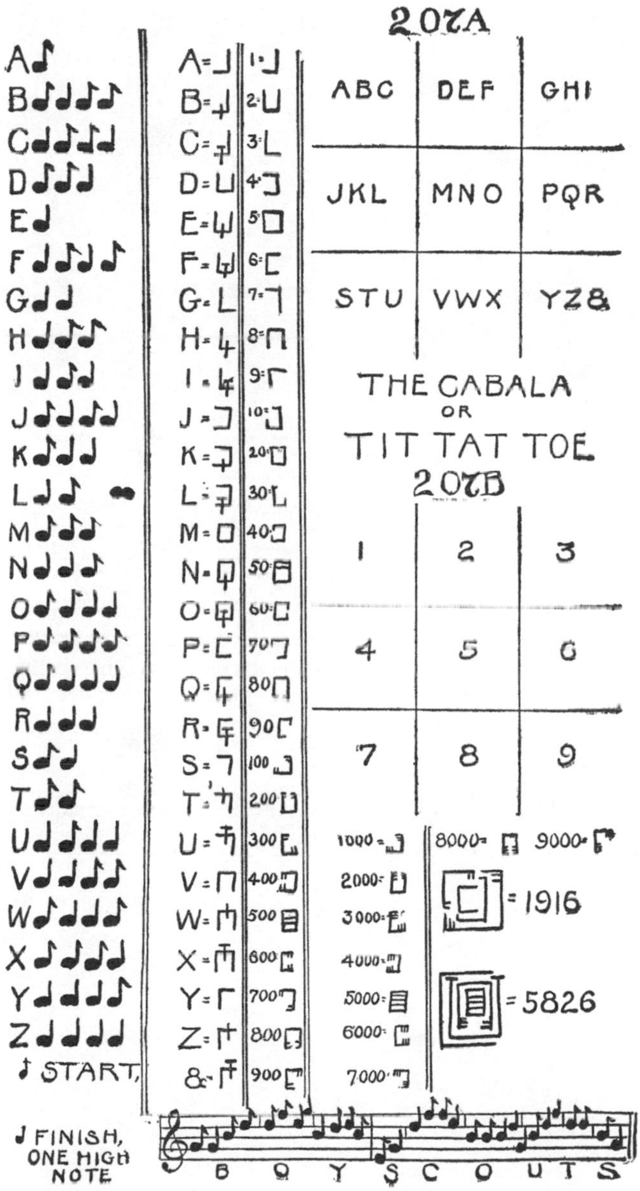
207A
A B C D E F G H I J K L M N O P Q R S T U V W X Y Z
START,
FINISH, ONE HIGH NOTE
A= B= C= D= E= F= G= H= I= J= K= L= M= N= O= P= Q= R= S= T= U= V= W= X= Y= Z= &=
1 2 3 4 5 6 7 8 9 10 20 30 40 50 60 70 80 90 100 200 300 400 500 600 700 800 900
ABC DEF GHI
JKL MNO PQR
STU VWX YZ&
THE CABALA
OR
TIT TAT TOE
207B
1 2 3
4 5 6
7 8 9
1000= 2000= 3000= 4000= 5000= 6000= 7000=
8000= 9000=
=1916
=5826
B O Y S C O U T S

would then be the same reversed " ⌐ "-shaped division with
single brackets on the ends of the lines and a hundred would
be the same with two brackets on the lines and a thousand
the same with three brackets on the line, as is shown in the
table below the diagram. With this method, if one wants
to write 1916, one combines the figures in any way to suit
one's fancy. In this instance the one thousand is first written
and assuming the top to be north, it forms the southeast
corner of the square, then nine-hundred is written which
forms the northwest corner of the square, this encloses the
characters for ten and six all of which reads 1916. Or, we
take the 5826. Since five thousand is the middle court
with three brackets it makes a good center piece and we
write that first. Over this we put the staple shaped eight
hundred with two brackets and around this we put the
U-shaped twenty with single brackets. Outside of this we
put the E-shaped six. To read any monogram of this kind
read it as you would ordinary numerals, that is, read the
thousands first, which in the last instance is five thousand,
next the hundreds, which is six hundred, and next the tens
which is twenty, and finally the units which is six, and the
whole of it reads 5826, but combined to make an ornamental
monogram which suggests to no one, not in the secret,
anything connected with numerals.

Secret Signs for Cost Marks

Some systems used by merchants are based on the
use of words containing ten letters, but with no two letters
alike; each letter then represents a numeral. Probably
the most popular, as well as the most venerable of these
words is our first President's name:

W A S H I N G T O N
1 2 3 4 5 6 7 8 9 0

This you see corresponds, letter for figure, with all the numerals up to ten. If the goods cost 75 cents they will be marked G I. If the cost is 29 cents, the mark will be A O, etc.

Another patriotic system is based on Lawrence's famous flag, "Don't give up the ship," which is abbreviated to:

D O N T G I V E U P
1 2 3 4 5 6 7 8 9 0

Another time-honored one is:

B Y E A N D K O S T
1 2 3 4 5 6 7 8 9 0

Any combination of words or one word with ten letters each differing from the others will do for a key. Of course there must be no duplicate letters in the word or words.

It is quite entertaining work to seek such words, for instance:

H Y D R A U L I C S
1 2 3 4 5 6 7 8 9 0

The Jeweler's Circular ten years ago said, "Such marks as these are no secrets if one sets oneself to pick them out. Usually all that is necessary is to find out what several of the ten letters are, and then select from among then the ones most likely to represent 1, 5 and 0. Such secret cost marks can be figured out in this way sometimes in five minutes. But customers seldom take the trouble to puzzle out these mystic signs."

Frequently a merchant uses the first letters of the alphabet, thus:

A B C D E F G H I J
1 2 3 4 5 6 7 8 9 0

Or as follows:

Z Y X W V U T S R Q
1 2 3 4 5 6 7 8 9 0

Or one may take every second letter in the alphabet or every third letter, beginning at either end.

An ideal cost mark, says a trade paper, is the one that has an easily remembered key; that may be transmitted by voice; that is so simple in form as to minimize chances of error in writing and reading, and one that is not what it seems to be. The following is an example: "1 2 3 4."

To use it: 1 doubles the figures placed after it, 2 adds 50 per cent to the figures placed after it, 3 deducts a third, 4 deducts a half. The cost mark key in this system is always the first or initial figure. Let us illustrate its use by an imaginary case.

In marking the cost on an article costing 60 cents, one may write it in four ways—130, 240, 390, 4120—as the initial. 1 means to double the following figures, the double of 30 is 60.

If the initial 2 adds fifty per cent then 50 per cent. of 40 is 20 and 20 added to 40 is 60.

The initial 3 means to deduct a third from the following figures, ⅓ of 90 is 30 and 30 from 90 is 60.

We have agreed that the initial 4 means to subtract one half, then in this case we have ½ of 120 is 60 and 60 from 120 is 60.

In writing the cost on the goods under this system the abbreviation NO. or the sign—is placed before the cost. Thus the customer is led to believe that it is the number of the article instead of the cost mark. This gives the seller a great advantage over the buyer. A conversation may be carried on between the clerk and the manager, or proprieter, before a customer, and the latter be none the wiser.

For instance, the customer is protesting against the price. The clerk may think a reduction wise, and that it will be granted by the manager, or he may desire the manager's indorsement of the price. In this case the manager does not have to examine the tag or ask its price to learn the cost. He simply says, "what number is it?" The letter of hieroglyphic system would not permit such simplicity in this case.

This same system can be used in games or in serious military work, for instance, the number of miles on a secret map or the number of men or batteries can be written in this manner and no outsider can understand the figures. A Scout sends word to his Chief of the number of men in front, the amount of ammunitions or other important items, and the numbers for the key are:

3 5 7 9

In this case 3 doubles the figures placed after it; 5 adds 50 per cent. to the figures placed after it: while 7 deducts a third and 9 a half, or any other arrangement agreed upon. If it is as indicated above and the Scout sends in

3 5 0 0 0

the Chief knows that it reads:

1 0 0 0 0

or it may be that 1 2 3 4 when placed in front of other numerals stands for the addition of one cipher, two ciphers, three ciphers, or four ciphers, then 1 3 5 0 0 0 would mean to add one cipher to the 3 5 0 0 and would read 3 5 0, 0 0 0 or 4 3 5, 0 0 0 or it would read 3 5 0, 0 0 0, 0 0 0. That is, there are three hundred and fifty million rounds of munition or population or that number of things sought.

CHAPTER XVII

NUMERALS OF THE MAGIC
Ancient System of Secret Numbers

At least so they are claimed to be by occult authors. You know that in ancient times religion, astronomy, medicine, and magic were all mixed up so that it was difficult to tell the beginning of one and the ending of the other and to-day the Gypsies, hoboes, free masons, astronomers, scientists, almanacs, and physicians still use some of the old magical emblems. So there is no reason why the boys of to-day should be debarred from using such of the signs as may suit their games or occupations and we will crib for them the table of numerals from old John Angleus, the astrologer. He learned them from the learned Jew, Even Ezra, and Even Ezra learned them from the ancient Egyptian sorcerers, so the story goes; but the reader may learn them from this book.

Fig. 207 C. The characters are divided up into units first from one to nine, all of which face the right. Then they are divided up into tens from ten to ninety; the same characters being used in each case but the tens face the left. Next they are turned upside down facing the right and are hundreds from one hundred to nine hundred. Still upside down but turned to face the left the characters make thousands from one thousand to nine thousand.

The root of these characters is the same as our letter "I" or the numeral "1." Now if we wish to make something of this root, to represent the unit "one" we put the bracket on the top extending to the right, for ten it extends to the left, consequently, if we make it like the letter "T," that is, extending to the right, which is one, and to the left which is ten, that will be eleven. Thus on this root you can build any sort of monogram up to four figures, as is shown in the table, that is, up to 9,999.

These are the characters which, used in connection with

FIG. 207C

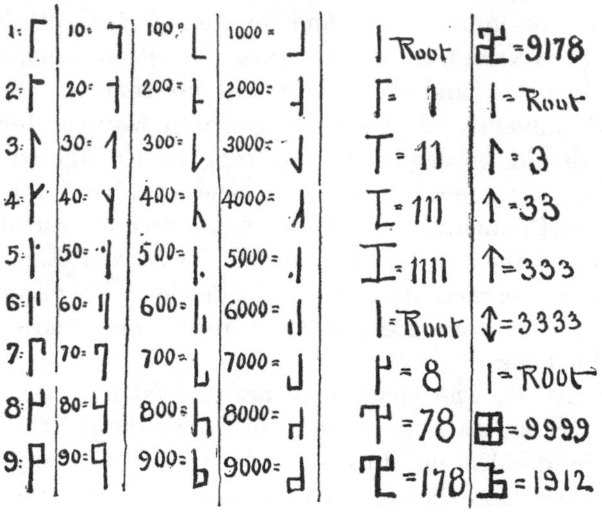

1: ⌐	10: ⌐	100: L	1000: ⌐	Root	=9178
2: ⌐	20: ⌐	200: ⌐	2000: ⌐	⌐ = 1	= Root
3: ⌐	30: ⌐	300: ⌐	3000: ⌐	T = 11	= 3
4: ⌐	40: Y	400: ⌐	4000: ⌐	= 111	= 33
5: ⌐	50: ⌐	500: ⌐	5000: ⌐	= 1111	= 333
6: ⌐	60: ⌐	600: ⌐	6000: ⌐	= Root	= 3333
7: ⌐	70: ⌐	700: ⌐	7000: ⌐	= 8	= Root
8: ⌐	80: ⌐	800: ⌐	8000: ⌐	= 78	= 9999
9: ⌐	90: ⌐	900: ⌐	9000: ⌐	= 178	= 1912

the Indian signs for months and days tell us the number of the month or day. The first month, of course, is January, and the first day is Sunday.

You are now equipped for writing long cipher dispatches which may not pass the censor because no censor is familiar with them and consequently will look upon them with suspicion.

The Use of Signs for a Map (207 D)

This figure shows a map of a wild bit of country. A
map of a tame bit of country would answer the purpose

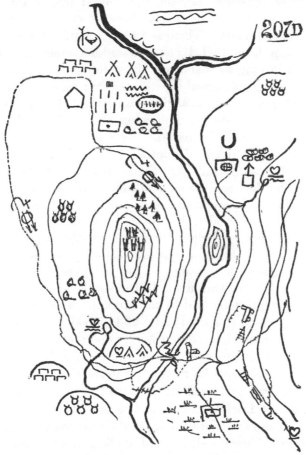

just as well but would not be as interesting. At the top of
the map there is a big body of water, a camp of redmen with
a drove of horses and food for man and beast. There is a

grove or forest of hardwood on the river bank near the camp. There are boats on the shore, probably canoes. There is danger at this camp which means that the redmen are hostile, but on the opposite side, the right hand side of the river, there is a good place to camp. Food is cached there, that means, hidden there. There is a cairn, or pile of stones, and three paces from that there is a hidden message. There is a trail leading to this camp along the shore of the river. There is a herd of horned beasts near by which are probably elk or caribou, for this is a wild country and there is no mark of ownership on them. Following the trail up the river but towards the lower part of the map we find that just above a swamp it meets another trail which, on the left, is marked an easy trail. On the right it intersects another trail which is four miles from a railroad to the north and three miles from a big water and a steam-boat to the south This is three miles of good trail. Going back to the easy marks we see that one trail runs down through the swamp and it is dangerous, probably a treacherous bog. But going west the trail runs over a bridge. This, however, has been destroyed and a new trail made to the south of it where there is a shallow place or ford in the stream. This leads up to our camp, which is a good camp and a good spring of water by it. There is a drove of our horses and our cattle near by. Our camp is on the side of a mountain or hill. There are sheep on the side of the mountain, probably Rocky Mountain Big Horns, and goats on the top of the mountain which are probably Rocky Mountain Goats. On the west side there is a hardwood forest and on the northeast side a pine or fir forest. There is also a herd of elk or deer of some kind on the northwest side of the mountain.

On each side of the mountain there is a trail shown by a dotted line, but on both trails at the north side of the mountains there is a command to halt and hit the trail back double-quick, which, no doubt, is because of the dangerous camp of redmen just beyond.

This map serves to illustrate how very, very useful these signs may be to the serious work of explorers, scouts and military men or the less serious play of the Boy Scouts.

A Cipher Letter

Figure 207 E. It seems to have been the custom of numerous primitive people to write their picturegraph letters

in a spiral. This we find in the ancient discs as, notably, the clay plate found in Crete and known as the Phaestos

Disc. Also we note the tribal histories of our own American Indians painted on buffalo hides in the same form.

So we will use a spiral for our letter (Figure 207 E).

In writing in a spiral you must, of course, begin at the centre, otherwise you could not calculate your space. Beginning at the centre here, we find that on the seventh day, or Saturday, of the sixth month, or June, 1916, the wind was blowing, it was raining with lightning. Through the rain four Scouts and a Scoutmaster passed, singing. The bridge was destroyed, the boats destroyed, and the Scouts were hungry. They forded the stream, still singing because ahead of them was a good camp, plenty of food, and a joyful heart.

This is a very simple form of letter. But almost anything that can be written on the type-writer may be told with our picturegraph signs gathered from the ancient astrologers, the hoboes and tramps, the explorers, surveyors, and American Indians.

COMPASS, MAGIC.

CHAPTER XVIII

GESTURE SIGNALS

Used by Boy Scouts, Military Men, Indians, Hunters, Cowboys, and Policemen

The idea of using gesture signals of the Indian as a universal language among the white people was first suggested by the writer to the American boys in various magazine articles and his books for boys. Since then others have taken

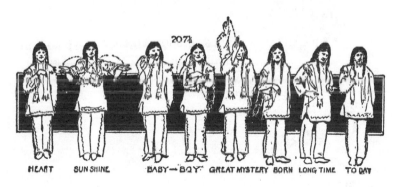

HEART   SUN SHINE   BABY—BOY   GREAT MYSTERY   BORN   LONG TIME   TO DAY

up the idea and developed it, so in place of writing an exhaustive book on gesture language, he has tried to select a few gestures for this book which are in use at the present time and which, if adopted by us all would make a short and simple system, easily understood and of practical service.

Fig. 207½. Indian gesture language for Merry Christmas, and is to be read "Sun shine in the heart a baby boy, Great Mystery, born on this day."

97

Fig. 208. Go back! Swing hand and arm around over the head. (Western hunter and plainsman signal.)

Fig. 208½. Go back! Retreat! Shoot your arm up then swing it down to your side. Keep doing this until order is understood. (Military signal.)

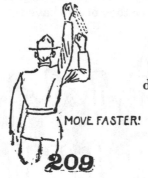

Fig. 209. Move faster; advance double quick. (Military signal.)

Fig. 210. Attention. Open hand held aloft, arm moved from right to left and left to right (about six inches) a number of times.

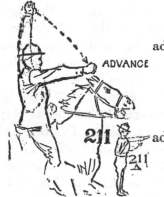

Fig. 211. March—go ahead—advance. (Military signal.)

Fig. 211A. March—go ahead—advance.

Fig. 211½. Come along—follow, according to the circumstances when it is used. Not so apt to alarm game as the more vigorous military signal. (Hunters in Africa and America.)

Fig. 212. Move to my left! Surveyors' signal which, reversed, would mean, move to my right. That this signal may be seen further, a surveyor sometimes holds a handkerchief in his hand and sometimes his hat in one hand and his handkerchief in the other.

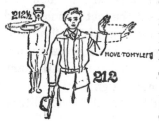

Fig. 212½. Go in this direction! column right! swing your hand from the shoulder across the body to the other side horizontally until the hand and arm is extended full length (Military signal.)

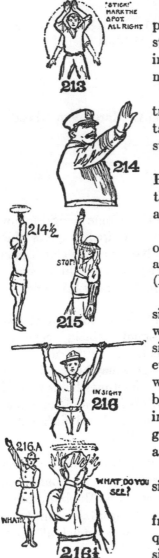

Fig. 213. You are at the right place—Mark it there—Hold your staff there. Signal used when placing a man in line usually the flagman. (Surveyors' signal.)

Fig. 214. Stop! Halt! Used by traffic policeman, also means stop talking; keep quiet. (Orators' and stump speakers' and traffic sign.)

Fig. 214½. Come here, assemble. Raise arm as in stop (Fig. 215). then draw imaginary circle on an imaginary ceiling over head. (Military.)

Fig. 215. Halt! Used by a lookout, the advanced guard or Scout as a command to his companions. (Hunters' sign.)

Fig. 216. I can see it—it is in sight—game is in sight—drinking water is in sight—our friends are in sight—the enemy is in sight. Whatever the Scout is sent to look for, when he sees it the fact is announced by holding his gun, his staff or fishing rod over his head horizontally, grasped by both hands. (Military and sportsman's sign.)

Fig. 216A. What? (Military signal.)

Fig. 216½. Open hand moved from right to left in front of eyes, a question, What see you? (Military sign.)

Fig. 217. Not in sight. Whenever the advanced Scout is unable to see the object of his search the fact is announced by his holding his Scout staff, his gun, his fishing-rod or other similar object upright at full arms' length above his head. (Plainsman's signal.)

Fig. 218. Caution—Be careful—Advance with care, look out for yourselves. Signal is made by holding the right hand up, the left hand down in a straight line with each other and slowly lowering the right hand and raising the left hand and repeating the motion three times. This may mean that there is a treacherous bog or a dangerous trail of any kind; it may mean dangerous animals, an ugly dog or a vicious bull.

Fig. 219. Nothing to fear—a friend, all clear. From a universal sign—throw up your hands—used to designate a safe trail or to say you are safe in coming this way, or I am a friend, I will not harm you; as the occasion may require. (Hold-up man's sign.)

Fig. 220. I have found it. When the party is sent in search of something, usually some object lost, if his search is successful he announces the fact by throwing a handful of dust in the air. (Gypsy, Hunters' and Boy Pioneer sign.)

I HAVE FOUND IT

Fig. 221. Stoop down—lie down—dismount! Hands and forearm extended in front of the body, hands then quickly moved downward, often accompanied by bending the body as the hands are moved downwards. (Hunters,' woodcrafters' and military signal.)

Fig. 222. Who are you? Index and second finger of each hand pointing forward and upward, arms sharply brought up to the height of the head with the fingers pointing up. (Western Indian sign or signal.)

DOWN WITH YOU! DISMOUNT

221

Fig. 223. A Scout. The wolf, to the Indians' minds is the greatest scout among the animals and the

222

WHO ARE YOU?

223

A SCOUT

224

AN AMERICAN,
A WHITE MAN.

gesture sign for a wolf is made by closing the fist with the exception of the first and second fingers; these are spread wide apart to represent the wolf's ears and the hand is held out about the height of the eyes and then moved forward with an up and down motion as if the animal were loping. The wolf being the scout among animals, the same sign is used for both wolf and Scout. This sign given in reply to the sign "who are you?" would mean "I am a Scout." (Indian sign.)

Fig. 224. An American—a white man—a "Boston" man. First doubled up thumb on the outside of the fingers, thumb placed over the eyebrow to the left side of the face, then drawn sharply across to the right as shown in the dotted lines in the diagram to indicate a hat brim; this in reply to the question "who are you?" would say, "I am an American—a white man—a Boston man"; among Indians represents a man from the East.

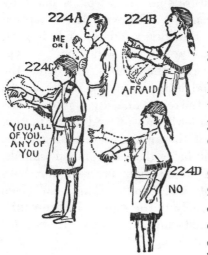

Fig. 224 A. Me or I.

Fig. 224 B. Afraid.

Fig. 224 C. You, all of you, any of you.

Fig. 224 D. No. No in Military signals is K of the semaphore code, while yes is P of the semaphore code.

Combination Figures 224 A, 224 B, 224 C, and 224 D; Defiance. Me afraid of all of you?   No! In other words, I am afraid of no one.   (Indian sign language.)

CHAPTER XIX

COMMON GESTURE LANGUAGE

In General Use by Civilized People, Boys, Merchants and the General Public

Hand Talk

Most people think that the gesture sign language is peculiar to the American Indians, but it was used by the ancient Egyptians as well as the Greeks and Romans during their greatest age of culture and enlightenment, and may still

be seen on the ancient vases. To-day it is a common mode of expression in Italy and very common here in the United States, for instance, we take the first hand sign (Fig. 225). This has always been among American boys used as the sign for swimming. It means "come and go a-swimming," "I am going a-swimming," or "are you going swimming?" according to the way in which one uses it.

In our first Boy Scouts' Society here in America, known as the Sons of Daniel Boone, before the English Boy Scouts was organized, the same position of the hand was used as a salute, or to indicate a scout; the hand was held up with the palm out, then moved with an up and down motion from the person, the fingers representing the ears of a wolf and the motion the loping action of that animal. The wolf, among Indians, being considered the scouting animal and typical of a Scout. When Baden-Powell, remodeled our

American Scout idea to fit the English boys, he added a third finger to the sign using the three fingers to stand for the three promises in the Scout oath.

Fig. 226. King's X, which means a truce. "Hold on a minute, I claim a rest." "It" cannot tag anyone when that one's fingers are crossed; this is a boy's sign. In ancient times the monastery and the King's house were both sanctuaries or retreats where even the criminal was safe from the law. The crossed fingers are called the King's X, or cross, probably because Church and State were united. This sign is also used to fend off bad luck. One must cross one's fingers and say "muggins" to protect one from the evil eye. The evil eye is an old superstition still prevalent in Italy and parts of France. Of course there is no truth in it.

Fig. 227. The closed fist. Shaking the fist, every boy knows what that means! It is a threat and means "I am going to beat you up—thrash you," or it may mean, "If you continue to do this or that thing, I will beat you." In that case, it is a threat combined with a caution.

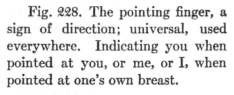

Fig. 228. The pointing finger, a sign of direction; universal, used everywhere. Indicating you when pointed at you, or me, or I, when pointed at one's own breast.

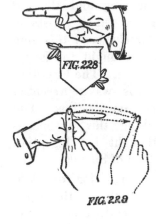

FIG. 228

Fig. 229. The sign of shame—shame on you—the forefinger of the left hand points at someone while the forefinger of the right hand is run down the other forefinger a number of times, as one would use a knife in whittling. All young people dread this gesture and old people do not love it when directed toward themselves.

Fig. 230. A sign of caution—tut-tut!— be careful! Principally used by parents and school teachers.

Fig. 231. Silence, keep quiet—mum! Finger against the mouth means the mouth is closed, and when the mouth is closed one cannot talk. The ancient Greeks used this sign for silence. It is used to-day by everyone. But with the ancient Egyptians it had

a different meaning and the old Greeks made a funny mistake, because the Greeks used this sign for silence they thought the Egyptians did the same. The Egyptian Dawn God, Horis, was represented with its finger on its lips. The Greeks mistaking this as meaning silence thought the Egyptian God was the God of Silence.

FIG. 232

Fig. 232. A sign for derision. Usually the thumb of the open hand, waving hand, touches the point of the nose. East of the Allegheny Mountains, this is generally, *but incorrectly*, associated with a low, vulgar expression. There is, however, nothing vulgar in the sign itself. It is usually directed to a person who has tried to "put something over" on one and failed. To a person who has tried to trap one into some ridiculous joke and the intended victim sees through the trap. The sign is used to let the joker know that his game is known. Also, if one is running and climbs out of reach of one's pursuer, the sign is used to show that the chase was a failure. Literally it means that the other party met with loss and disappointment, by a palm's breadth.

FIG. 233

Fig. 233. You are making a fool of yourself, hands at ears wagging back and forth representing the ears of a jackass.

FIG. 234

Fig. 234. Meaning that the one using it has succeeded in making a dupe, by fooling or deceiving another party. Place the fingers between the collar and the neck and rub the neck with the back of the hand, which tells your accomplice that the other party swallowed your yarn, or fish story, whole. In boys' comical and expressive slang. "They did not tumble to the game."

FIG. 235

Fig. 235. A humorous sign means "You can't fool me—I understand your game—the joke is not new—I have heard it before.

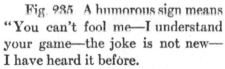

FIG. 236

Fig. 236. Pulling down the lower lid of the eye is sometimes used in a similar manner to Fig. 235, but it really indicates a cheat, a swindler, a fake. Finger under the eye, if one uses this sign and points to another boy, then it is a warning to look out for that boy, because he is not square, not honest. If it is used directly to the person talking with one it means "You can't fool me;" "go tell it to the marines" —"I see thru your joke, story or game." Usually in America it is used jestingly, but in Italy it is used seriously.

Fig. 237. Palm of the hand facing outward, waved back and forth rapidly, in front of the lower part of the face. Negative sign, "No, no. I cannot listen to you. Stop, quit that—cut it out."

Fig. 238. Ta-ta! Good-bye, farewell, a sign known by every child. Also used as a greeting, salute, meaning "How-d'ye do, and goodbye." Used in this manner from a car window or passing vehicle.

Fig. 239. Yes, I agree with you. The forefinger of the right hand joining the middle of the cushion of the finger with the end of its own thumb, moderately extending the rest of the fingers. This means "yes," among the people of Naples and other parts of Italy. Practically the same among the American Indians. A sign of approval—good —all right—O. K.

Fig. 240. Boy Scout's salute and sign. English, adapted by the famous Baden-Powell from the Indian sign of "scout" (Fig. 223) used by the Sons of Daniel Boone,

the first boy scouts here in America. The English sign does not stand for a Scout as such, as did the original American sign still used by the Boy Pioneers, but it stands for the principles of Scouting, the three things in the scout oath; First finger, honor God and country; Second finger, help others; Third finger, obey the Scout law. This is now also used by the Boy Scouts of America and the Boy Scouts all over the world.

Fig. 241. Money. A common sign used by shop-keepers, gamblers, and people in general. This is made by rubbing the end of the thumb and the fore or index-finger together, indicating the picking up and counting of money. Sometimes used as a demand to pay your score —pay up, I want the money—or meaning "I will comply with your request if you pay me cash."

There are many signs used in every-day life which are so familiar to us, such as nodding the head for yes, shaking it for no, and shrugging the shoulders when in doubt, that we fail to recognize how great a part gestures play in ordinary conversation.

Every religious body and secret society employs a regular code of hand signs, but the American Indian after all is the one who has the most complete conversational set of gestures. Next to him come the Neapolitan Italians.

CHAPTER XX

HAND ALPHABETS, DEAF AND DUMB ALPHABETS
CURB NUMERALS AND NEUROGRAMS

THERE is nothing new or novel regarding the alphabets used by the deaf and dumb people, but these hand alphabets have always been a source of great interest to young people

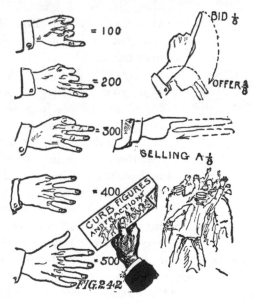

and properly have a place in this book of Signs, Signals and Symbols. The author has arranged them so that the two-handed alphabet is placed opposite the one-handed alphabet thus, the letter A of the one-handed plan is opposite the letter A of the two handed plan, etc. The diagrams explain themselves.

To these well known alphabets has been added a system of numbers and fractions used by stock brokers, especially on "the curb" at Wall Street, these signals (Figs. 242 and 243) may be very useful to scouts, auctioneers and military

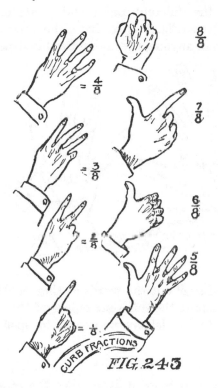

$$\frac{8}{8}$$

$$= \frac{4}{8}$$

$$\frac{7}{8}$$

$$= \frac{3}{8}$$

$$\frac{6}{8}$$

$$= \frac{2}{8}$$

$$\frac{5}{8}$$

$$= \frac{1}{8}$$

CURB FRACTIONS

FIG. 243

men. For instance, the commander wants to know how many men are hidden in the woods, the scout holds up his hand with all except the little finger closed, and the commander immediately knows there are a hundred men out there; thus there are innumerable ways in which these figures and fractions may be of service to people outside of Wall Street.

Mrs. Ella Bennett of Denver, Colorado, was born deaf and mute; being threatened with blindness she invented

A New System of Hand Letters

by assigning the different parts and joints of the hands to different letters (Fig. 244) so that altho a person was deaf, dumb and blind, anyone, by taking the blind person's hand

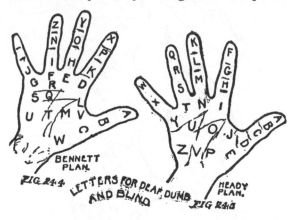

in theirs, could spell out the words as they could on a typewriter by touching the different points of the hands which corresponded to the letters necessary to spell the words. This is called

Neurography

or nerve writing, because it is all thru the sense of feeling that she reads what is spelled out to her upon her hand. For instance, if you are blindfolded and someone touches with their fingers the tip of your thumb you immediately know that the letter is A, because the tip of your thumb is A, and the sensitive nerves in your thumb have telegraphed to your brain instantly the exact spot that the finger touched.

THE DEAF AND BLIND POET OF KENTUCKY

Morrison Heady fashioned himself a glove with the alphabet on it (Fig. 245), but the arrangement of the letters on it are somewhat different from those that Mrs. Bennett made; each of them, however, seem to have selected certain nerve centers for the letters. Mrs. Bennett marked the letters on her hand with an indelible pencil so that her friends might talk to her, the old blind and dumb poet had the letters marked upon a glove. When he pulled this glove upon his hand his friends could talk to him by touching the letters marked upon the glove.

But for secret communications boys can learn the location of these letters upon the hand just as my stenographer has learned on the type-writer and is now taking, direct, by dictation what I am saying, and doing it as rapidly as I talk.

In order to do this with one's hand, it is best to adopt the poet's method of marking up a glove first, and practicing with that glove until one can do it with one's eyes closed; it will then take a very little time for two boys, for instance, to be able to talk to each other by holding hands, or talk to each other from quite a distance by holding up one hand (Fig. 246) and touching

FIG. 246

the points representing the letters with the forefinger of the other hand as shown in the diagram. This is a new way for scouts to signal, which will seem almost magical to the on-looker.

Understand, that by first lettering the hand or glove

and practicing upon that, you will learn the location of the letters just as quickly as you could upon a type-writer, so that after you can talk to another expert by touching the points on the bare hand, which you have learned to know correspond with said letters; thus what these two unfortunate people invented thru their necessity, we may use for-fun or more serious reasons. This system, if understood by military men, might be of the greatest practical service in conveying secretly messages from one to the other.

The Ordinary Deaf and Dumb Alphabets

These are either one or two hand letters. That is, one alphabet is composed of letters made with one hand and the other is made by a combination of two hands. Inasmuch as these alphabets are explained in the diagrams it is unnecessary to explain them in the text, neither is it necessary to number each letter; hence they will appear under one general number Fig. 247.

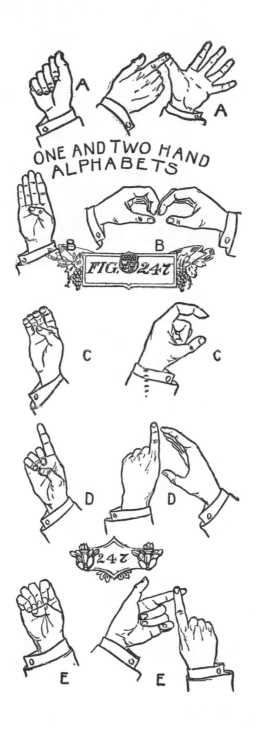

ONE AND TWO HAND ALPHABETS

FIG. 247

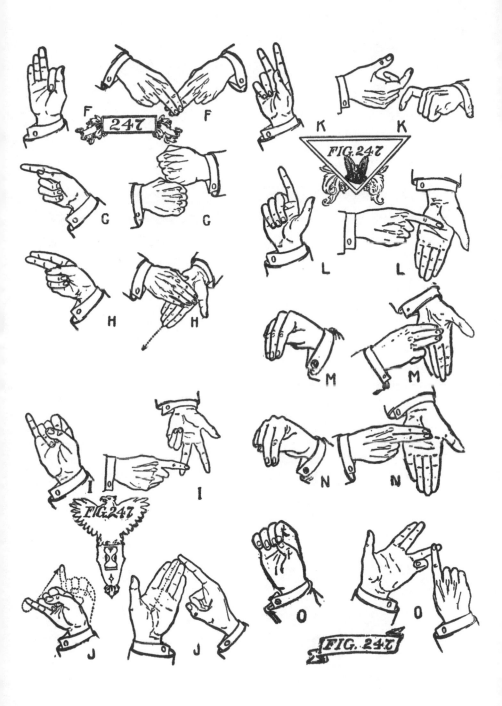

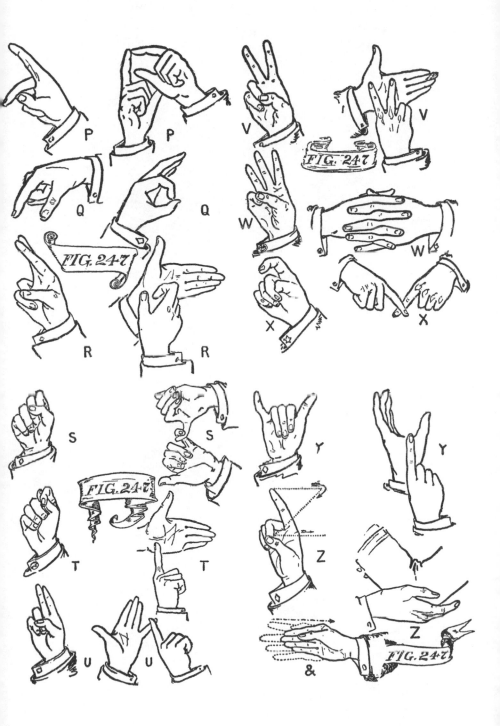

CHAPTER XXI

SIGNAL CODES

INTERNATIONAL MORSE CODE OF DOTS AND DASHES; AMERICAN MORSE CODE, DOUBLE FLAG SIGNALING; ARDOIS SYSTEM OF LIGHTS; PERMANENT HOISTS SYSTEM OF FLAG SIGNALING BY REFLECTORS, HELIOGRAPH AND SEMAPHORE SIGNALS

SOME boys find it difficult to memorize the dot and dash system used in telegraphing. In order to overcome this difficulty, Lieutenant James H. Beard of the 2nd Field Artillery, New York National Guard, made up a chart of small animals to illustrate each letter for my outdoor school of woodcraft, and the pupils used the Lieutenant's method very successfully.

Memorize the name of the animals which represent each letter (Fig. 249). The names of the animals will bring to mind the way they are pictured and the pictures will recall to you the arrangement of dots and dashes.

This method is now in use at the Dan Beard Outdoor School.

GENERAL SERVICE CODE (Fig. 249)

A—Ant and adder—a dot and a dash.

B—Bat and bees—a dash and three dots.

C—Crows—dash, dot, dash, dot.

D—Duck—a dash and two dots.

E—Egg—a dot.

F—Fish—two dots, a dash and a dot.

G—Geese—two dashes and a dot.

H—Hares—four dots.

I—Ibex—two dots.

J—Jaybird and jackals—a dot and three dashes.

K—Kangaroes—a dash, a dot and a dash.

L—Larks and lizards—a dot, a dash and two dots.

M—Monkeys—two dashes.

N—Narwhals—a dash and a dot.

O—Owls—three dashes.

P—Penquins and pelicans—a dot, two dashes and a dot.

Q—Quails—two dashes, a dot and a dash.

R—Rats and rhinoceros—a dot, a dash and a dot.

S—Snapping turtles—three dots.

T—Turkey—a dash.

U—Unicorns—two dots and a dash.

V—Vultures—three dots and a dash.

W—Walrus—a dot and two dashes.

X—Xiphiidæ (swordfish)—a dash, two dots and a dash.

Y—Yaks and yellowhammers—a dash, a dot and two dashes.

Z—Zebras—two dashes and two dots.

Fig. 248 shows the numerals.

FIG. 248
NUMERALS

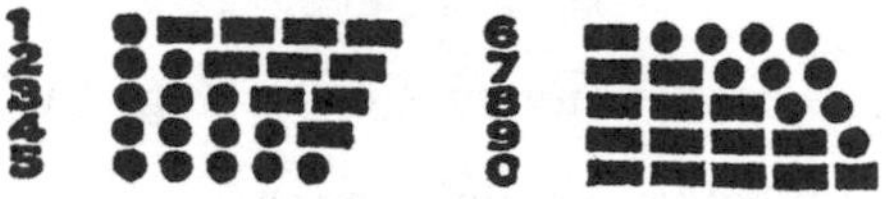

FLAG SIGNALING

It is extremely popular with the boys and a knowledge of it and proficiency in sending messages is part and parcel of Boy Pioneers' and Scouts' education, as well as that of the Girl Pioneers, Girl Scouts and Camp Fire Girls. Signaling should also be taught in all the public schools because the drill with the flags is an excellent exercise, is interesting and the knowledge gained is most practical and useful.

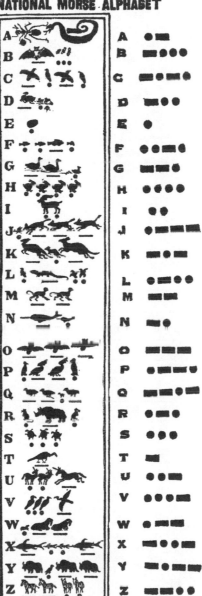

Fig. 249

SEMAPHORE

The post with movable arms known as the semaphore is authorized for general use by the Army. The stationary short arm on the right-hand side (of the sender) is called the indicator (Fig. 250) and it tells one at a distance which way the sender is facing and thus makes it possible to read the signals. An examination of the diagram will convince the reader of the necessity of knowing the right arm from the left arm, thus the indicator tells the observer the position of the sender. The arms of the semaphore are used in sig-

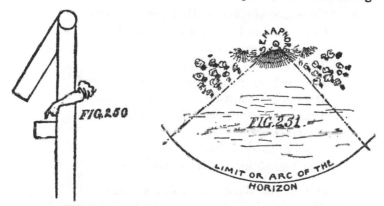

nalling exactly as the arms of a man when doing the same service, the semaphore of course, is set at a point where it may be seen the greatest and also the widest distance, or to put it more scientifically the semaphore is set at a point "so situated that it may be seen through the greatest arc of the horizon" (Fig. 251).

There are many semaphores established on the French, Italian, Portuguese coasts and some on the Spanish and Austrian coasts, where only the International code of signals are now used. Where practicable these semaphores have means of communication by telegraph with each other and with the Chief metropolitan lines and foreign stations.

Passing ships are able to exchange communications with the semaphores, and when required their messages are forwarded to their destination according to the fixed tariff. On the coasts of Great Britain, there are signal stations which offer the same facilities to passing vessels.

The semaphore is extensively used to-day by railroad employing the block system and Alice Lovett Carson speaks graphically of the railroad semaphore as—

"Guarding the trains that pass our door,
Over the track stands the semaphore:
Great long arms that move in air
Tell of safety or danger there:
Outward pointing: 'a train's gone by.'
Downward slanting: 'no danger nigh.'
Trainmen, scanning the distance o'er,
    Glancing on high,
    Note, as they fly,
The signaling, silent semaphore.

"Out in the dark, when day's asleep,
The semaphore lanterns twinkle and peep;
Each great arm has a blinking eye
To wink at the trains as they rumble by:
Red: 'take care, there is danger near!'
Green: 'go ahead, for the track is clear.'
Trainmen know of this color lore,
    Glancing on high
    At the warning eye
Of the winkety, blinkety semaphore."

The vanes of the official semaphore are painted yellow. Sometimes these machines are fitted out with electric lights to be used after dark. The arms on railway semaphores are painted different colors. (See sketch over title to diagram of hand signals, flag and lamp signals, Figs. 285, 286, 287, etc.)

The dot and the dash may be used wherever sound or motion can be heard or seen. While the author was acting as Chief of a large camp of Boy Scouts he allowed the guests at the council fire to take two of his boys, gag them, tie their hands behind them and bind up their feet and in this helpless position they were cast down near the council fire and about thirty feet apart facing each other, then one of the visitors whispered a message in the ear of one of the boys stretched prone upon the ground in front of the council fire. After a few moments the gag was removed from the second woodcrafter and he repeated the message of which no one but the two directly concerned had any knowledge. How is it done? Very simply. The boy who sent the message did so by winking his eyes, a short wink for a dot and a long wink for a dash.

Afterwards the same boys were blindfolded put BACK to BACK and again the experiment was tried and again the message was repeated correctly. How was it done this time? Why, when they were placed back to back the Chief so arranged them that their hands, which were tied behind their backs as you remember, touched each other and thus by the wiggling of the finger of one boy on the hand of the other boy, the message was transmitted.

Some unthinking persons may ask of what practical use is this knowledge? A mining engineer is imprisoned by a cave-in in the mine, but his rappings are heard by the rescuing party and if he knows how, he can telegraph messages to those outside and direct their efforts at rescue work. Also business men can talk thus without being overheard and the possibilities among military men is unlimited.

The Ohio floods gave us a condition where the signaling with flags, a hat or a handkerchief, would have been of immense service in saving life and property had the victims of the high waters who were marooned on the housetops possessed a knowledge of signaling.

The flags used by the United States Army for hand signaling are 18 inches square and divided diagonally into two parts, one red and the other white. The flag staffs are two feet long. The Field and Coast Artillery use a hand flag of orange with a scarlet centre and scarlet with an orange centre; these flags also are 18 inches square, with a centre of 9 inches by 9 inches and the staff two feet long.

Red and white are colors used by surveyors because they are readily seen at a distance. Red may be obscured on a background of foliage, but the dark foliage will make the white stand out more distinctly. The white may not be noticeable against the light sky, but the light sky will make the red stand out very distinctly.

Some years ago, never mind how many, the writer belonged to a rowing club, the rowing shirts' colors were purple and orange stripes, at a distance of less than a quarter of a mile the purple was not distinguishable at all; in other words the orange was so much stronger than the purple that it carried further, just as some sounds which appear loud when close by are not distinguishable at a distance while others have great carrying powers; hence the probable use of orange by the Field Artillery, orange being a strong color.

Single Flag Signaling

To signal by dots and dashes, first stand at "position" (Fig. 252) with the flag staff held perfectly erect and right in the middle of the body and along the line of the nose. Of course, the sender must directly face the receiver or the

station with which he is to talk. A dot is made by bringing
the flag down to the right side (Fig. 253), opposite the middle
of the body and back again to its upright position, the dash
is made by doing the same thing on the left side. (Fig. 255).

To indicate a pause or the end of a sentence bring the
flag down directly in front of you and immediately back
again, upwards to its first position, (Fig. 254). With these
three motions every word in Webster's unabridged dictionary

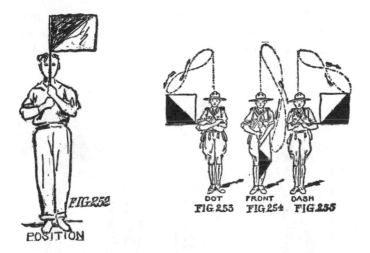

FIG.252

POSITION

DOT   FRONT   DASH
FIG.253   FIG.254   FIG.255

may be spelled, including all of those in all the other dic-
tionaries. To attract attention when you want to signal
to a person or station make a signal of a dot (Fig. 253) and
dash (Fig. 255) at intervals until it is answered. Of course,
if it is a regular station and you know its call you give the
dot and the dash, then give the particular call required by
that station. To answer a call or to let them know that you
have noticed their signal, give a dot (Fig. 253), a dash (Fig.
255) and a dot (Fig. 253).

Flash Light Signal's Call

If you are using a light with no shutters, flash the light first directly overhead, that is straight up in the air, then swing it across at right angles to the line between you and the station in a half circle, or 180 degrees; keep doing this until you get a reply.

Double Flag Signaling

By reference to the accompanying diagrams it may be seen that the hand flags are used exactly the same as the wooden arms of the semaphore machine for all the letters, but in marking an interval (Fig. 256) the flags are crossed

INTERVAL'   FIG. 256   ATTENTION FIG 258   NUMERLS TO FOLLOW FIG. 257

in front of the sender's legs and where numerals are to follow, the flags are crossed directly over the sender's head (Fig.257).

"Numerals" (Fig. 257) precede every number sent and indicates numerals until "interval" (Fig. 256) is made, after which letters recur without any further indication. When numerals follow letters no intervening "interval"

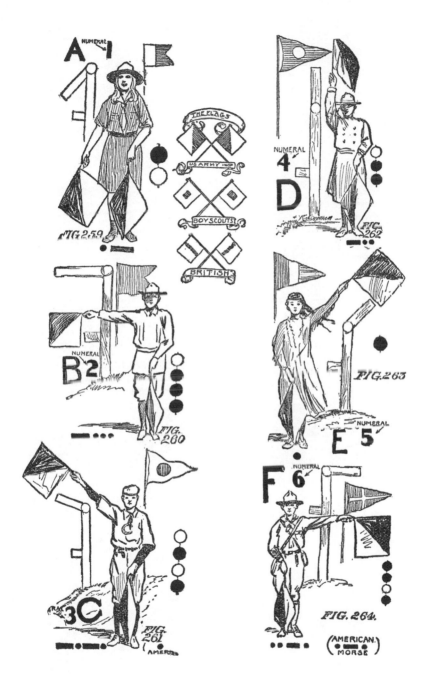

NUMERAL
A 1

THE FLAGS

U.S. ARMY

BOY SCOUTS

BRITISH

FIG. 259

NUMERAL
4
D

FIG. 262

NUMERAL
B 2

FIG. 260

FIG. 263

NUMERAL
E 5

NUMERAL
F 6

3 C

FIG. 261

AMER 26

FIG. 264.

AMERICAN.
MORSE

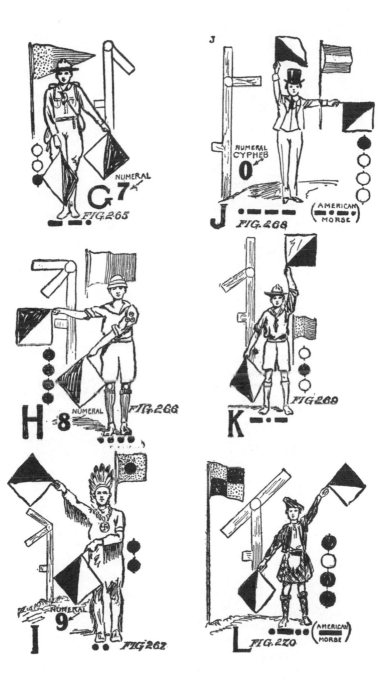

G 7 NUMERAL FIG. 265

J NUMERAL CYPHER **0** FIG. 268 (AMERICAN MORSE)

H 8 NUMERAL FIG. 266

K FIG. 269

I 9 NUMERAL FIG. 267

L FIG. 270 (AMERICAN MORSE)

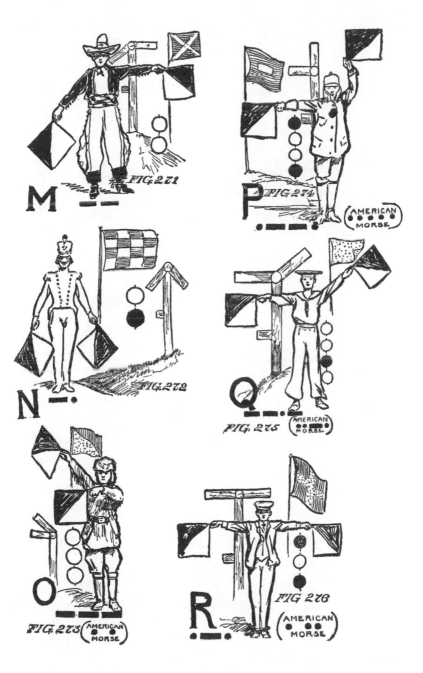

M ▬ ‥

FIG. 271

N ▬ ·

FIG. 272

O ‥ ▬
FIG. 273 (AMERICAN MORSE)

P · ▬ ▬ ·
FIG. 274 (AMERICAN MORSE)

Q ▬ ▬ · ▬
FIG. 275 (AMERICAN MORSE)

R · ▬ ·
FIG. 276 (AMERICAN MORSE)

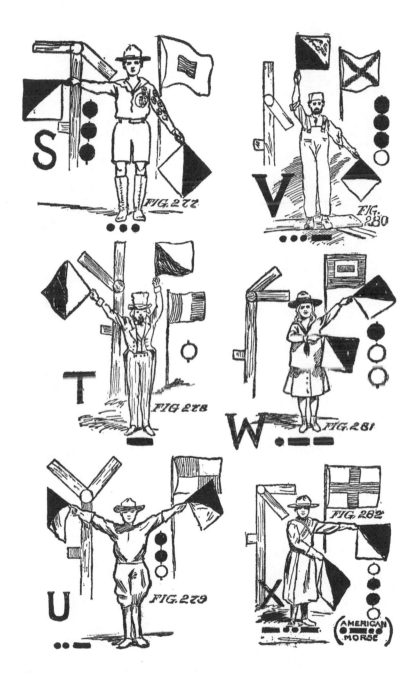

S

FIG. 277

V

FIG. 280

T

FIG. 278

W

FIG. 281

U

FIG. 279

X

FIG. 282

AMERICAN
MORSE

is necessary. When communicating with the Navy, numerals are spelled out.

With the exception of the interval, hand flags are used practically in the same way as is the semaphore.

POSITION

Face the station squarely when calling it (Fig. 252), and if you get no response to signal, wave the flag overhead and try again until you get a reply.

THE INTERVAL

is signalled by crossing the flags downward (Fig. 256) just above the knees in front of the body. The double interval is made by giving the chop, chop signal twice, and the triple signal by giving the chop, chop three times.

By examining the following diagrams the reader will notice that the right-hand flag starts up at A, is half way up at B, three-quarters the way up at C and all the way up at D. At E the signaller changes his hand and E is one-quarter the way down, F is half-way down and G three-quarters the way down. After G we begin over again with the right hand flag, holding it in the same position we did at B; but from "H" to "J" the left hand flag *is not* held in the same positions that it was in "B," "C," and "D."

The numbers are shown by the first ten letters of the alphabet that is "A" is 1, "B" is 2, "C" is 3, "D" is 4, "E" is 5, "F" is 6, "G" is 7, "H" is 8, "I" is 9 and "J" is 0. "K" is used for no or negative, "N" for annulling or cancelling. "O" for question or interrogatory and "U" for attention. In assuming this last position, to attract attention the flags are shaken with an up and down movement. (Fig. 258). "R" is used for acknowledgment.

FIG. 283. FIG. 284.

EMERGENCY SIGNALS FOR USE ON CABLE AND TELEGRAPH LINES

Rule 71 of the Signal Book of the United States Army for 1916 says: "The general attention or emergency call for use on cable or land telegraph lines is the numeral "9." It will be sent out only by the proper authority and will have its meaning clearly understood. Upon hearing the call all operators will give way, but they will remain at their instruments until relieved. They will not cut in unless called. The numeral "9" is an emergency call; it may be used in anticipation of attack or riot; it may be used to indicate a conflagration or other danger and should be used only in case of need. This signal is of great importance and should be thoroughly understood by all cable and telegraph operators. It should be conspicuously posted with appropriate instructions, as to its meaning and use, in all cable and telegraph stations.

THE HELIOGRAPH

The heliograph system is signalling with a piece of bright tin or looking-glass in the sun or with flash lantern or a search light equipped with a shutter. A short flash is, of course, a dot and a long one is consequently a dash; make the long flash steady and a trifle longer than one would use with a "ticker" for the sound.

"A" is the universal call signal and is always used unless another signal is known for the station call.

At sight of the call signal, the stations will turn on a steady stream of light and adjust their apparatus; when ready the called station will douse its glim, as the ancient sailors used to say, in other words, shut off their light, upon which the other party will transmit his message.

Whenever anything goes wrong with the lamps or reflectors of the sender the receiver turns on a steady stream of lights and awaits a similar signal as an assurance that all is right and the talk may continue. Upon receiving the required assurance that all is right, the receiver cuts off his light and the message is continued.

The steady stream of light means either wait a minute for me or I will wait a minute for you, according to the way it is used.

When using any of the conventional signals as a question, follow the signal with the "question mark," that is the interrogation signal which is used in signalling as is the ? in writing. Thus if Q R Q is the command to send faster, Q R Q followed by the interrogation will mean, shall I send faster?

The Ardois System

The Ardois system is a display of four lights which are used as dots and dashes. Red light is a dot, while a white light is a dash. Usually these lights are electric bulbs swung from a mast, yard or pole of some kind. The lights are worked by a key-board.

The last ten letters of the alphabet are used as numbers in the Ardois system, thus Q is 1, R is 2, S is 3, T is 4, etc., to Z which stands for naught or cipher.

W, W, W, W is known as the cornet and used as a general call, the call is answered by W, W, W, W. But if the personal call of a particular station is known, then that call is used and is answered with the same call. When the lamps are placed in a row that is one beside the other or horizontally they must be read from the *sender's* right to the *sender's* left and consequently this is reversed for the receiver as he is facing the sender and his left hand is opposite the sender's right hand. When the lights are hung, one below the other as they are shown in the diagrams (Fig. 259 to 284 inclusive) they must read from the top down.

The Ardois, the semaphore, and the hand flag signal and the permanent hoist (Flag) are shown on each of the accompanying diagrams. Each figure is made differently in order to break the monotony of the diagrams as well as to help the pupil to fix the signal in his mind; the writer did not, however, put the sailor boy at S, as he did a Zouave at Z, this was done purposely on the theory that the breaking of so evident and natural order, like the reading of a book upside down, would mildly shock the mind and make a more lasting impression than if the expected arrangement were there.

American Morse

Wherever the American Morse differs from the more generally used International the characters are placed in brackets and marked "American Morse" on the diagrams.

Flags

PERMANENT HOISTS

The International Code of signals consists of 26 flags, a flag for each letter of the alphabet and they are all shown in their proper order along with the semaphore and hand-flag diagrams. The colors of the flags are indicated by the engraved lines on them according to the rules shown by Figures 160 to 166 inclusive.

CHAPTER XXII

BELL, ROPE AND WHISTLE RAILWAY SIGNALS

IN the Ohio Valley and all along the river banks down the great Mississippi River, all the boys of yesterday knew the steamers by the sound of their whistles, as well as by the set and decoration of their smoke stacks; it was a favorite trick with the lads to pretend to possess phenominal eyesight. Whenever they were fortunate enough to have a tenderfoot in the crowd, one wise boy would remark, "Say, Billy," what boat is that coming round the bend?" "That?" the other would reply, "why Sam can't you read, what's the matter with your eyes? That is the—I can hardly read it myself—let me see M-a-g-n-o-l-i-a, Magnolia!"

"So it is," Sam would chime in, altho at the distance the boys were from the steamer it would have taken a powerful telescope to have made the letters visible, yet when the steamer would approach sufficiently near for human eye sight to decipher the name on the paddle box, the tenderfoot could see "Magnolia" as plain as day, and he would be filled with astonishment and look at Sam and Bill with awe.

Neither Bill's nor Sam's eyesight, nor any other human being's eyesight for that matter, was good enough to read that name when the boys first pretended to spell it out, but these boys knew the Magnolia's whistle; not only that, they knew her smoke stacks and the reading of the names was only a make-believe. Since those good old days of river travel, everybody travels by rail in the southwest as well as in the east.

145

Vast armies of commuters live in the country surrounding all our big cities and all these people who travel by railroads are more or less interested in the meaning of the railway toots here given.

If we represent a short toot by a dot and a long one by a dash then, according to the Rule Book of the American Railway Association, the commonly used signals will appear as follows:

A number of short angry toots is the signal of danger ahead, it warns the trainmen that cattle, people or vehicles are on the tract ($\cdot\cdot$ $\cdot\cdot$ $\cdot\cdot$)

Toot!   Stop—put on brakes ($\cdot$)

To-o-o-o-o-t ⎫
To-o-o-o-o-t ⎬ Release brakes (— —)

To-o-o-o-o-t ⎫
Toot   ⎪
Toot   ⎬ Flagman, go back and protect rear of train.
Toot   ⎭   (— $\cdot$ $\cdot$ $\cdot$)

To-o-o-o-o-t ⎫
To-o-o-o-o-t ⎪ Calls the flagman back from west or south.
To-o-o-o-o-t ⎪   (— —— — —)
To-o-o-o-o-t ⎭

To-o-o-o-o-t ⎫
To-o-o-o-o-t ⎪
To-o-o-o-o-t ⎬ Calls the flagman back from east or west.
To-o-o-o-o-t ⎪   (— —— — — —)
To-o-o-o-o-t ⎭

To-o-o-o-o-t ⎫
To-o-o-o-o-t ⎬ When running, train parted; to be repeated
To-o-o-o-o-t ⎭   until answered. (— —— —)

Toot ⎱ Answer to any signal not otherwise provided for.
Toot ⎰   (· ·)

Toot ⎫
Toot ⎬ When train is standing. Back! (· · ·)
Toot ⎭

Toot ⎫
Toot ⎪
Toot ⎬ Call for signals. (· · · ·)
Toot ⎭

To-o-o-o-o-t ⎫ To call the attention of trains of the same or
Toot ⎬ inferior class to signals displayed for a fol-
Toot ⎭ lowing section. (— · ·)

To-o-o-o-o-t ⎫
To-o-o-o-o-t ⎪ Approaching public crossing at grade.
Toot ⎬   (— — · ·)
Toot ⎭

To-o-o-o-o-o-o-o-o-t ⎱ Approaching stations, junctions and
⎰ railroad crossings at grade. (——)

CHAPTER XXIII

RAILROAD, HAND-FLAG, LANTERN RAILWAY SIGNALS

IT would indeed be a sign, signal or symbol of a total lack of imagination and curiosity on the part of any traveller who viewed the hundreds of colored lights in a railway yard without feeling some desire to understand what these lantern were talking about.

It is evident to the most casual observer that they are talking and also that the engineers on the incoming trains understand their blinking and winking language.

Every small boy is deeply interested in the actions of the railway employees whenever they appear with lanterns or flags in their hands. And that we are able to here give the reader an inkling to what these flags mean and how to use them is due to the courtesy of an official of the old Erie Railway who kindly supplied us with the general rules used by all the railways and from these rules the following signs, symbols and signals were selected as being the ones most necessary to understand.

RAILROAD, HAND FLAG AND LANTERN SIGNALS

(ADOPTED APRIL 24, 1901)

NOTE: The hand, or a flag, moved the same as the lamp, as illustrated in the following diagrams, gives the same information or command.

Fig. 285. Stop—Swung across the track.

Fig. 286. Proceed—Raised and lowered vertically.

Fig. 287. Back—Swung vertically in a circle (half arm length) across the track, when the train is standing.

148

Fig. 288. Train Has Parted—Swung vertically in a circle at full arm's length across the track, when the train is running.

Fig. 289. Apply Air Brakes—Swung horizontally in a circle when the train is standing.

Fig. 290. Release Air Brakes—Held at arm's length above the head when train is standing.

The red flag (Fig. 291) is a signal to stop. It is a command which may not be disobeyed.

The blue flag is used for protecting workmen. A blue flag (Fig. 292) by day and a blue light by night, displayed at one or both ends of an engine, car or train, indicates that workmen are under or about it. When thus protected it must not be coupled to or moved. Workman will display the blue signals and the same workmen are alone authorized to remove them.

The green and white flag (Fig. 293) is a flag stop. The combined green and white signal is used to stop a train only at the flag stations indicated on the schedule of that train. When it is necessary to stop a train at a point that is not a flag station for that train, a red signal is used.

RAILWAY SEMAPHORE

A vertical position of the blade or a white light means safe. A horizontal position of the blade or a red light is a sign of danger and intermediate position of the blade or a green light demands caution. See sketch with the title of Hand Flag and Lamp Signals, over Figs. 285–6–7, etc.

RAILROAD TRAIN AND ENGINE SIGNALS

(ADOPTED APRIL 24, 1901)

NOTES: On diagrams, G is green, R is red, W is white. The diagrams are intended to illustrate location of the train signals, not the exact manner in which they are to be attached.

Combination lamps with four illuminated colored faces are represented in the diagrams.

ENGINE RUNNING FORWARD BY DAY AS AN EXTRA TRAIN

White flags at A A. Extra trains will display two white flags and, in addition, two white lights by night, in the places provided for that purpose on the front of the engine (Fig. 294).

ENGINE RUNNING FORWARD BY NIGHT AS AN EXTRA TRAIN

White lights and white flags at A A. Extra trains will display two white flags and, in addition, two white lights by night, in the places provided for that purpose on the front of the engine (Fig. 295).

ENGINE RUNNING BACKWARD BY DAY AS AN EXTRA TRAIN WITHOUT CARS OR AT THE REAR OF A TRAIN PUSHING CARS

White flags at A A. Extra trains will display two white flags and, in addition, two white lights by night, in the places provided for that purpose on the front of the engine.

Green flags at B B, as markers. The following signals will be displayed, one on each side of the rear of every train as markers, to indicate the rear of the train: By day, a green flag. By night, except when the train turns out to be passed by another and is clear of main track, when a green light must be displayed to the front (Fig. 296).

ENGINE RUNNING BACKWARD BY NIGHT AS AN EXTRA TRAIN WITHOUT CARS OR AT THE REAR OF A TRAIN PUSHING CARS

White lights and white flags at A. A Extra trains will display two white flags, and in addition, two white lights by night, in places provided for that purpose on the front of the engine.

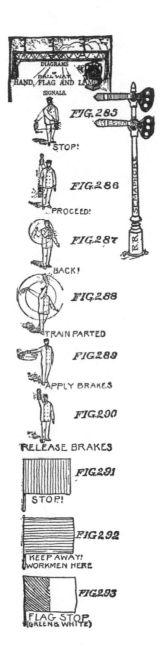

DIAGRAMS
OF
RAILWAY
HAND, FLAG AND LAMP
SIGNALS.

FIG.285

STOP!

FIG.286

PROCEED!

FIG.287

BACK!

FIG.288

TRAIN PARTED

FIG.289

APPLY BRAKES

FIG.290

RELEASE BRAKES

FIG.291

STOP!

FIG.292

KEEP AWAY!
WORKMEN HERE

FIG.293

FLAG STOP
(GREEN & WHITE)

Lights at B B, as markers, showing green at side and in direction engine is moving and red in opposite direction. The following signals will be displayed, one on each side of the rear of every train: By day, a green flag. By night a green light, to the front and side and a red light to the rear, except when the train turns out to be passed by another and is clear of main track, when a green light must be displayed to the front, side and to the rear (Fig. 297).

ENGINE RUNNING FORWARD BY DAY DISPLAYING SIGNALS
FOR A FOLLOWING SECTION

Green flags at A A. All sections of a train, except the last will display two green flags and, in addition, two green lights by night, in the places provided for that purpose on the front of the engine (Fig. 298).

ENGINE RUNNING FORWARD AT NIGHT DISPLAYING SIGNALS
FOR A FOLLOWING SECTION

Green lights and green flags at A A. All sections of a train, except the last will display two green flags and, in addition, two green lights by night, in the places provided for that purpose on the front of the engine (Fig. 299).

ENGINE RUNNING BACKWARD BY DAY WITHOUT CARS, OR AT
THE REAR OF A TRAIN PUSHING CARS, AND DISPLAYING
SIGNALS FOR A FOLLOWING SECTION

Green flags at A A. All sections of a train, except the last will display two green flags and, in addition, two green lights by night, in the places provided for that purpose on the front of the engine.

Green flags at B B, as markers. The following signals will be displayed, one on each side of the rear of every train, as markers, to indicate the rear of the train: By day a green flag. By night a green light to the front and side and a red light to the rear, except when the train turns out to be passed by another and is clear of main track, when a green light must be displayed to the front, side and to rear (Fig. 300).

ENGINE RUNNING BACKWARD BY NIGHT WITHOUT CARS, OR AT THE REAR OF A TRAIN PUSHING CARS, AND DISPLAYING SIGNALS FOR A FOLLOWING SECTION

Green lights and green flags at A A. All sections of a train, except the last, will display two green flags and, in addition, two green lights by night, in the places provided for that purpose on the front of the engine.

Lights at B B, as markers, showing green at side and in direction engine is moving and red in opposite direction. The following signals will be displayed, one on each side of the rear of every train, as markers, to indicate the rear of the train: By day a green flag. By night a green light to the front and side and a red light to the rear, except when the train turns out to be passed by another and is clear of main track, when a green light must be displayed to the front, side and to rear (Fig. 301).

REAR OF TRAIN BY DAY

Green flags at A A, as markers. The following signals will be displayed, one on each side of the rear of every train, as markers, to indicate the rear of the train: By day, a green flag. By night, a green light to the front and side and a red light to the rear, except when the train turns out to be passed by another and is clear of main track, when a green light must be displayed to the front, side and to rear (Fig. 302).

REAR OF TRAIN BY NIGHT WHILE RUNNING

Lights at A A, as markers, showing green toward engine and side and red to rear. The following signals will be dis-

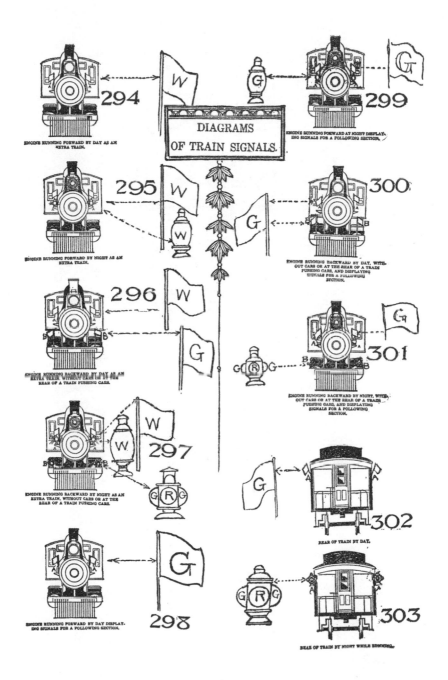

DIAGRAMS
OF TRAIN SIGNALS.

294

ENGINE RUNNING FORWARD BY DAY AS AN
EXTRA TRAIN.

295

ENGINE RUNNING FORWARD BY NIGHT AS AN
EXTRA TRAIN.

296

ENGINE RUNNING BACKWARD BY DAY AS AN
EXTRA TRAIN, WITHOUT CARS OR AT THE
REAR OF A TRAIN PUSHING CARS.

297

ENGINE RUNNING BACKWARD BY NIGHT AS AN
EXTRA TRAIN, WITHOUT CARS OR AT THE
REAR OF A TRAIN PUSHING CARS.

298

ENGINE RUNNING FORWARD BY DAY DISPLAY-
ING SIGNALS FOR A FOLLOWING SECTION.

299

ENGINE RUNNING FORWARD AT NIGHT DISPLAY-
ING SIGNALS FOR A FOLLOWING SECTION.

300

ENGINE RUNNING BACKWARD BY DAY, WITH-
OUT CARS OR AT THE REAR OF A TRAIN
PUSHING CARS, AND DISPLAYING
SIGNALS FOR A FOLLOWING
SECTION.

301

ENGINE RUNNING BACKWARD BY NIGHT, WITH-
OUT CARS OR AT THE REAR OF A TRAIN
PUSHING CARS, AND DISPLAYING
SIGNALS FOR A FOLLOWING
SECTION.

302

REAR OF TRAIN BY DAY.

303

REAR OF TRAIN BY NIGHT WHILE RUNNING.

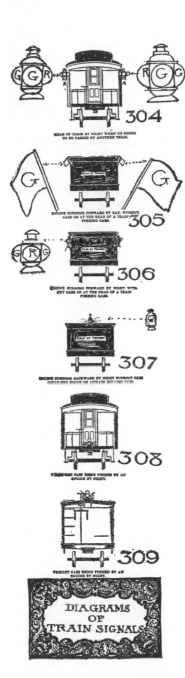

304

REAR OF TRAIN BY NIGHT WHEN ON SIDING
TO BE PASSED BY ANOTHER TRAIN.

305

ENGINE RUNNING FORWARD BY DAY, WITHOUT
CARS OR AT THE REAR OF A TRAIN
PUSHING CARS.

306

ENGINE RUNNING FORWARD BY NIGHT, WITH-
OUT CARS OR AT THE REAR OF A TRAIN
PUSHING CARS.

307

ENGINE RUNNING BACKWARD BY NIGHT WITHOUT CARS
OR AT THE REAR OF A TRAIN PULLING CARS.

308

FREIGHT CARS BEING PUSHED BY AN
ENGINE BY NIGHT.

309

FREIGHT CARS BEING PUSHED BY AN
ENGINE BY NIGHT.

DIAGRAMS OF TRAIN SIGNALS

played, one on each side of the rear of every train, as markers, to indicate the rear of the train: By day, a green flag. By night, a green light to the front and side and a red light to the rear, except when the train turns out to be passed by another and is clear of main track, when a green light must be displayed to the front, side and to rear (Fig. 303).

REAR OF TRAIN BY NIGHT ON SIDING TO BE PASSED BY
ANOTHER TRAIN

Lights at A A, as markers, showing green toward engine, side and to rear. The following signals will be displayed, one on each side of the rear of every train, as markers, to indicate the rear of the train: By day, a green flag. By night, a green light to the front and side and a red light to the rear, except when the train turns out to be passed by another and is clear of main track, when a green light must be displayed to the front, side and to rear (Fig. 304).

ENGINE RUNNING FORWARD BY DAY, WITHOUT CARS OR
AT THE REAR OF A TRAIN PUSHING CARS

Green flags, as markers. The following signals will be displayed, one on each side of the rear of every train, as markers, to indicate the rear of the train: By day, a green flag. By night, a green light to the front and side and a red light to the rear, except when the train turns out to be passed by another and is clear of main track, when a green light must be displayed to the front, side and to rear (Fig. 305).

ENGINE RUNNING FORWARD BY NIGHT, WITHOUT CARS OR
AT THE REAR OF A TRAIN PUSHING CARS

Lights at A A, as markers, showing green to the front and side and red to rear. The following signals will be displayed, one on each side of the rear of every train: By day, a green flag. By night, a green light to the front and side and a red light to the rear, except when the train turns out to be passed by another and is clear of main track, when a green light must be displayed to the front, side and to rear (Fig. 306).

ENGINE RUNNING BACKWARD BY NIGHT, WITHOUT CARS OR AT THE FRONT OF A TRAIN PULLING CARS

White light at A (Fig. 307).

PASSENGER CARS BEING PUSHED BY AN ENGINE BY NIGHT

White light on front of leading car. When cars are pushed by an engine (except when shifting or making up trains in yards) a white light must be displayed on the front of the leading car by night (Fig. 308).

FREIGHT CARS BEING PUSHED BY AN ENGINE BY NIGHT

White light on front of leading car. When cars are pushed by an engine (except when shifting or making up trains in yards) a white light must be displayed on the front of the leading car by night (Fig. 309).

TORPEDO SIGNALS

Railroad men ofttimes signal to oncoming trains by affixing torpedoes to the rails which are exploded when coming trains run over them.

One torpedo—signal to stop.

Two torpedoes—not more than 200 feet apart is a signal to reduce speed and a caution to look out for a stop signal.

"Heaps," "Lots" many torpedoes—not official, but it is a recognized signal, and all railroad men know by the continuous reports and exploding torpedoes that there is a bride and groom on the train and that the groom is a railroad man.

It may sometimes be quite important for passengers to know the

BELL ROPE SIGNALS.

There are occasions of accident when a passenger might save serious consequences by quickly using the bell rope signals. At the same time no passenger should ever touch the bell rope except on occasions of great emergency, for a sudden stop by the train may itself produce an accident, consequently the rule is to let the railroad official attend to that duty except in emergencies where moments count and no time can be lost without dire results.

Two pulls on the bell rope is a signal to start when train is standing.

Two pulls on the bell rope, when train is running, is a signal to stop at once.

Three pulls on the bell rope, when train is standing, is a order to back the train.

Three pulls on the bell rope, when train is running, is an order to stop at next station.

Four pulls on the bell rope, when train is standing, is an order to apply, or release air brakes as the case may be.

Four pulls on the bell rope, when train is running, is an order to speed.

Five pulls on the bell rope, when train is standing, is to call in the flagman.

Five pulls on the bell rope, when train is running, is a signal to increase speed.

CHAPTER XXIV

STEAMER TOOT TALK

Including International and General Steering and Sailing Rules; Secret Language of Toots

General Prudential Rule

In obeying and construing these rules, due regard shall be had to all dangers of navigation and collision, and to any special circumstances which may render a departure from the rule necessary in order to avoid immediate danger.

The SOS of radio telegraphy is well known to everyone as an emergency signal. SOS is composed of three letters, three of anything, we have seen, is the usual sign of danger or alarm and in this case is a distress signal used at sea. It is international and is the universl sign or call for help. Not only should its meaning be thoroughly understood by all radio operators and wireless men, but its explanation should be posted everywhere where there is a station which could be of any assistance. Appropriate instruction should also be printed on the poster. Rule 73 of the Signal Book of the United States Army says: "The operator of any army radio station aboard ship, upon receiving an SOS signal, will immediately ascertain the exact position in latitude and longitude of the vessel sending the signal. When the information has been received the operator will immediately have the same delivered to the officer in charge of the ship, who will take the necessary action."

General Steering and Sailing Rules

GENERAL PRINCIPLES

All of the following rules are based upon the rules of the road with which all drivers are familiar and which are governed by one very simple principle, which is, that every vehicle, be it wagon, automobile or steamboat, must keep to the right. At sea or in harbor a steamer in passing another steamer whether in meeting or in crossing, MUST KEEP TO THE RIGHT, or, in other words, must present her own port side to the vessel which she is passing. Red is the color of port wine and also the color of the port light. Port is the left side when one is facing the bow with back to stern. The starboard is the right side when one is facing the bow, green is the color of the right side or, starboard light.

Toot-Talk

THE MEANING OF SHORT AND LONG TOOTS

When a boat, particularly a ferryboat, is coming out from its slip it gives one long blast on its whistle.

You boys in the interior may not understand this because the ferryboats do not have slips there. They have wharf boats, and since the wharf boats do not conceal the ferry it is not always necessary for them to give warning when they leave the wharf. Around New York, upon the inlets of the sea, or straits, improperly called "rivers" the docks which the ferries use often have piers frequently and improperly called "docks" on both sides. The piers usually have buildings upon them, which conceal the ferryboat from the vessels in the open water; consequently it is necessary for the ferries to give warning when they come out of their dock or slip, otherwise they might pop out right in front of a passing steamer or sailing vessel or go crashing into the side of one without any warning.

It is probably true that in every port in the United States there is a brotherhood or branch of the American Association of Masters and Pilots of steam vessels. This association is said to be a secret order, but anyone who is a licensed master may become a member. This association as a matter of course has its own private pass words and "high signs" and otherwise resembles other secret societies. But it differs in one respect and that is its members are said to have

A Secret Language of Toots

By their toots, they are known, and a brotherhood man need but listen to the whistle of a steamer to not only learn if it is in charge of another brotherhood man but also to what particular lodge, camp or group the master belongs.

These signals are not intelligible to the outsider, but the regular members soon learn to talk toot-talk to each other as they go puffing around the harbor and people on the shores hear them and know that they are talking; but few, if any, know what they say except when they use the universal whistle signals which govern the movement of steam vessels everywhere and prevent collision and disaster.

This much outsiders claim to have learned. A long blast of the whistle (—) followed by a short one (·) or (— ·) means "Are you one of us?" If the reply is one long blast (—) followed by two short ones (· ·) or (—· ·) it is translated as "Yes, sir, I am."

This much settled the "brothers" toot, toot to each other information about the tides, tows or other marine matters of interest to tugboat men, pilots and steamboat masters.

There is another signal with which even the newspapers seem to be familiar and that is the

BROTHERHOOD DISTRESS SIGNAL

And it is claimed that it always brings an answer if there is another steamer within hearing; the signal is *One long blast, one short one, then another long one and another short one,* that is (———— ·———— ·). This signal appears to be the "Hey Rube" of the steamboat men. "Hey Rube" is the old rally call of the circus men when there was a fight in view with the townspeople or farmers.

OTHER PRIVATE SIGNALS

Everywhere, especially around New York, the ferry-boats and busy self-important tug-boats have private signals of their own by which they can convey necessary information to each other and to the men on the barges which may be in tow. These private signals are not in the Brotherhood code, the International code or the Government code and may be only temporary signals used by pre-arrangement between the captain, for instance, of a tugboat and the crew of the barges in tow. Each barge has its number and the attention of the crew is instantly obtained when it hears the number of that particular barge called. Attention obtained, the tugboat captain issued orders by the pre-arranged toot signal, but these signals can be of no practical use to the reader.

The ordinary signals, however, used by all steamboats are a source of constant interest to all intelligent passengers whether they be boys or only ordinary grown folks. For the convenience and fun of it we have named the steamers in the following diagrams after the months and days.

SOUND SIGNALS

KEEP TO THE RIGHT

Let us suppose that the steamers January and February are apparently bound to meet bow on, to prevent a collision it will of course be necessary for these vessels to change their courses or direction. Since the rules of the road require us to keep to the right, January gives one long blast (—) which says, "I will turn to the right," February answers with one blast (—) which means, "so will I," and thus they pass each other safely (Fig. 310).

When the vessels are apparently going to meet bow on, and (Fig. 311) both swerve to the right, it will bring their port sides facing, or opposite, each other; supposing it is night time then both pilots, as they approach each other, can see the red (port) and green (starboard) lights of the opposite vessel, thus telling each that they will meet bow on unless their courses are changed, but when they each swerve to the right only the red may be seen from either vessel.

> "When both lights you see ahead,
> Port your helm and show your red.'

It is only when breaking the general rule that two blasts are given (— —).

Fog Signals

The International rules require the following signals to be sounded at intervals not exceeding 2 minutes.

(—) a long blast is from four to six seconds.

(·) a short blast is one second.

Steamboats with engines stopped tell others where they are by giving one long blast, one second interval and another long blast (— —).

Sailing vessel moving by aid of sails (that is underway), and on the starboard tack, signal with one long blast (—) on the fog horn.

On port tack, two long blasts (— —).

Wing and wing, with wind abaft beam, sailing free, three long toots (— — —).

Vessel towing, being towed or not under command or vessel working with telegraph cable, one long toot and two short toots (— · ·).

Vessel fishing, one long toot (—) or ring a bell for five minutes.

Vessels at anchor ring a bell five seconds.

U. S. Inland rules, at intervals not exceeding 1 minute.

Vessel at anchor, ring bell rapidly for 5 seconds (at intervals of 1 minute.)

Vessel fishing, one long blast (—). Ring bell.

SOUND SIGNALS
FOR VESSELS IN SIGHT OF EACH OTHER

One short toot (·) means, I am directing my course to starboard. (Fig. 310)

Two short toots (· ·) means, I am directing my course to port. (Fig. 312)

Three short toots (· · ·) means, my engines are going full speed astern.

> "From three short blasts 'tis yours to learn
> That she's going full speed astern."

VESSELS MEETING END-ON

Alter course to starboard:

Helm to port: Each, one long blast (—).

> "If one whistle you should blow,
> To starboard then your bow must go.
> And speeding across the tide.
> She'll pass to port along your side."   (Fig. 311.)

VESSELS COMING TOWARD EACH OTHER FROM OPPOSITE DIRECTION

Each turn to the right, one toot and one toot for an answer (—). (Fig. 311.)

Helm to starboard:

Each two long blasts (— —).

"If two whistles you should blow,
Why then to port your bow must go.
And if the space is fair and wide,
You'll pass along her starboard side." (Fig. 312.)

"JULY" CROSSING AHEAD OF "AUGUST"

August slackens speed if necessary and July keeps her course and speed. One long blast (—). (Fig. 313.)

"OCTOBER" CROSSING AHEAD OF "SEPTEMBER"

October keeps her course and speed and September slackens speed if necessary. Two long blasts (— —). (Fig. 314.)

OVERTAKING VESSELS

If December has come up from more than two points abaft November's beam, December must keep clear. December slackens speed if necessary.

But if December comes up directly astern (Fig. 315) of November and wishes to pass to the right she signals with One Toot, if she wishes to pass to the left she signals with Two Toots; in doing this she is asking permission of November, and if November consents she answers with the same signal, but if for some reason she does not want December to pass her on that particular side she gives not less than four rapid toots, which means, No! no! you cannot pass me on that side (Fig. 315).

VESSELS CROSSING

Both backing— "Monday" crossing ahead of "Sunday:"
"Sunday" keeps clear while "Monday" crosses ahead, one long blast (—). (Fig. 316.)

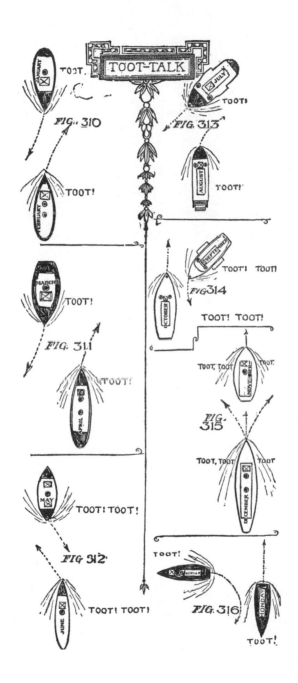

TOOT-TALK

TOOT.

FIG. 310

TOOT!

FIG. 311

TOOT!

TOOT!

TOOT! TOOT!

FIG 312

TOOT! TOOT!

TOOTS!

FIG. 313

TOOT!

TOOT! TOOT!

FIG 314

TOOT! TOOT!

TOOT, TOOT!   TOOT.

FIG. 315

TOOT, TOOT   TOOT

TOOT!

FIG. 316

TOOT!

Both backing—"Tuesday" crossing ahead:

"Wednesday" keeps clear. Two long blasts (— —). (Fig. 317.)

"Friday" going ahead—"Thursday" backing:

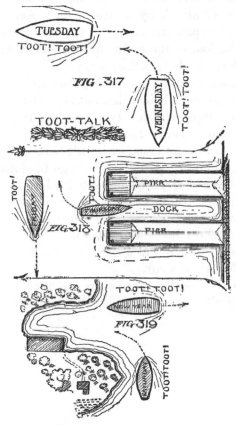

"Thursday" keeps clear. One long blast (—). (Fig. 318.)

"New Year" backing—"Saturday" going ahead:

"Saturday" keeps clear. Two long blasts (— —). (Fig. 319.)

SUBMARINE ALARM!

When the Cunarder "Carmania" arrived from Liverpool, we learned exactly what the signal is, and what passengers and members of the crew must do on a British liner in the event of attack by a submarine. According to the newspapers, a typewritten copy of the new instructions was posted at the foot of the main companionway of that vessel when she docked. It tells the story:

This signal is from a morning paper and at this writing is not in any printed official rules, but is probably correct:

Signal on ship's whistle—two long and two short blasts. Ship is being chased or in danger of gunfire. (— — · ·).

Passengers will go to boats with life belts on.

Seamen told off for gun's crew will go to stations.

Remainder will prepare the boats for lowering.

Firemen and trimmers will double up the watches in stokehold and engine room and raise all possible steam. All bulkhead doors being kept closed.

Remainder of men will go to their boat stations or put out fires when they occur.

Surgeon will see that all sick are removed.

Safety of all depends upon the strict observance of these rules.

CHAPTER XXV

WEATHER SIGNS

Told by Color of Sky, Direction of Wind, Cloud Effects, Fog and Dew; Signs Wise and Otherwise

When the Sea Calls

Some men are said to be called by the sea; a certain note in its moaning has a special significance to the English longshoreman and when they hear it a change comes over them, some becoming silent and sorrowful while others turn to dissipation and drown their dread in drink.

On certain parts of the Cornwall coast sailors dread walking at night near those portions of the shore where there have been many wrecks, for they firmly believe that the souls of drowned sailors haunt such localities and further affirm that the calling of the dead has frequently been heard. Indeed, at night time, on approach of a storm these callings are declared to be of common occurrence and many a sailor positively asserts that he has heard the voices of the dead sailors "calling their own names." There is also a legend said to have originated with the American Indians, to the effect that when the lake makes a noise like the booming of the Indians' tom-toms or drums it is announcing the death of someone, presumably a canoeist or sailor or a number of people as the case may be.

There is, however, another "calling of the sea" that has a different significance for it is heard far inland and is said to foretell a change in the wind and also the direction from which it will blow. This is what Edward Fitzgerald, who loved the sea and the ways of the men of the sea, described as "a kind of prophetic voice from the body of the sea itself announcing great gales; and Tennyson refers to it where he writes.

> "There came so loud a calling of the sea
> That all the houses in the haven rang."

And Glenn Ward Dresbach, here in America, has evidently heard the call of the ocean too, and it appeals to him like the call of the wild does to the Camp-fire man for Dresbach sings:

> "But the more I know of the ocean,
>   The more it calls to me,
>   Filling my soul with longing
>   Akin to misery."

Preceding snow storms old North Shore, Long Island, people hear the roar of the ocean all the way across Long Island, newcomers hear it too, if they are awake early enough, but they do not know the sound and mistake it for the noise of the city. But in Flushing, immediately preceding the great blizzard, the ocean could be heard booming upon the south shore as distinctly as if it had been but a few yards distant.

It is a remarkable coincidence that after writing the above the author awoke the next morning at 3:20 o'clock and heard the breakers distinctly; when he arose at 7 o'clock the first snow of the season began to fall. It is only early in the morning that the sea may be heard, because later in the day the rumble of wagons, trucks, trains and automobiles drowns the sound of the ocean. In inland towns the weather-wise folks predict rain when the distant railway trains are heard.

When the English longshoreman sees "water dogs," that is small dark clouds in the sky, he knows that wet weather is coming and when he speaks of "Winnol weather" he means the boisterous kind of weather generally experienced at the beginning of March, about the time of the anniversary of the British Saint Winwaloe.

Many years of observation and study of thunder storms

FIG. 320 SHOWING HOW STORMS FOLLOW REGULAR TRAILS

in three different states convinces the writer that these noisy rude summer guests have well-defined trails from which they seldom wander (Fig. 320), but when they do, oh my! hold down your tent, close your shutters and doors, or if you are in the open seek shelter because something is very liable to happen.

At the author's camp in Pike County, Pennsylvania, the thunder storms all come from the west side of the lake a trifle south of west, and travel a little north of east. Since 1887 only three times has this rule varied, and each of these times the storm came with a whoop and a yell from the northwest.

But so conventional are the thunder storms, as a rule after one has been observed on the darkening western hori-

AN AEROPLANE VIEW OF AN IRREGULAR STORM *FIG 321*

A CUMULUS CLOUD *FIG 322*

zon, it is almost possible to stake out the exact road the storm is to travel (Fig. 320). Also one is able to tell within a few minutes just how long it will be before the rain begins to fall. If the storm is of irregular form, (Fig. 321) the man at E may think himself safe, but when the wing of the storm comes he will get wet. Figure 320 shows three separate storms and where they will strike at A–B–C and D.

Very large cumulus clouds (Fig. 322) often precede violent storms and such clouds seldom, if ever, appear without an electric display. Often one of these heavenly super-dreadnaughts will sail along discharging its bolts of lightning with the system and regularity of a well-handled battleship.

A "weather breeder" in the daytime is a day "when

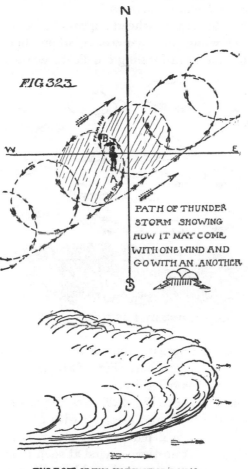

FIG. 323.

PATH OF THUNDER
STORM SHOWING
HOW IT MAY COME
WITH ONE WIND AND
GO WITH AN ANOTHER.

THE BORE OF THE ON RUSHING SQUALL
FIG. 324.

distant objects appear nigh," as it is expressed, or when the atmosphere is so crystalline and clear that the background seems to be jammed up against the foreground. At night when the stars appear extraordinarily numerous and brilliant it is also a "weather breeder."

When the blue sky overhead appears to be washed with a thin coat of white, in other words, when there is a thin mist away up overhead forming a delicate white veil known

.THE MAXFIELD PARRISH CLOUDS. NW WIND·

as cirropallium, it foretells rain, A northwest wind in the summer brings clear weather, (Fig. 323). As a rule it tells us that the storm has rolled by.

Thus a man at B–A (Fig. 323) sees the storm come apparently from the S.W. and clear up with a wind from the northwest, altho the real path of the storm is from southwest to northeast. A northwest wind at such times is almost invariably accompanied by a clear blue sky covered with drifting, woolley, small cumulus-like clouds with white backs

and dark bellies like those Maxfield Parrish loves to paint
(Fig. 325).

Cirrus Clouds

The white whisps of clouds five or six miles above the
earth are the cirrus clouds, their sudden appearance in the
clear summer sky indicates foul weather, especially is this
true when the ends of their feathers turn upward (Fig. 326),
showing that the clouds are falling. Rain in two or three
days follows the appearance of cirrus clouds.

If the raindrops in place of drying, cling to the leaves and
twigs there will probably be more rain. Late in the day
when the sun is observed shining thru a gray haze it will
rain at night, and when the moon is encircled by a ring or

MACKEREL SCALES ..

A MARES TAIL   FIG. 326

rings, the rings tell us that we may expect rain, for the
rings are caused by the moon shining through the cirropallium
already mentioned. When dark-colored small clouds hurry
along below the big clouds that means rain. When the
ground is dry and no dew appears on the grass in the morning
it betokens rain. When the clouds overhead are thick and
gray with a lumpy uneven lower surface, like the inverted
tops of a pan of biscuits or buns (Fig. 327), look out for a
steady rain. When little whirlwinds of dust, leaves or bits
of paper occur, it is said to foretell rain.

Whistling is thought very unlucky by sailors, as it is
supposed to raise an unfavorable wind. This superstition is, perhaps, to be traced to the practice of whistling

for winds, common to many nations in days gone by. A whistling woman is a sure sign ? to a sailor of coming disaster, wreckage and so on.

The moon and clouds also play an important part in a

THE BISCUIT CLOUDS   *FIG.327*

sailor's life and the notion that the weather changes with the moon's quarters is firmly implanted in his mind.

> "I saw the moon last yester-e'en,
>   With the old moon in her arms;
> And if we go to sea, master,
>   I fear we'll come to harm."

A rainbow in the morning shows that the shower is west of us and that we will probably get it; but a rainbow in the evening shows that the shower is east of us and that means it has passed over.

> "A rainbow at night
> Is the sailor's delight;
> But a rainbow in the morning
> Sailors, take warning!"

Fine weather is predicted by mottled sky, while a mackerel sky gives warning of wind or rain.

"Mare's tails and mackerel scales
Make lofty ships carry small sails." (Fig. 326)

On a windy night, we need fear neither dew nor frost. Dew is the heaviest after a hot day. Three days of frost is generally followed by rain.

Anvil-shaped clouds announce the coming of a gale.

Did you ever notice that some days foul odors, as well as sweet ones are more noticeable, flowers more fragrant and smoke descends instead of rising? This foretells rain.

Fog forming in the morning brings us a fair day. Fog settling during the night is (it is claimed by many) very very sure to bring us a misty, rainy day; but this is not as reliable a rule, for the day after the fog is often fine.

Here are some signs that old-fashioned housewives prefer to the barometer. There is some truth, and a lot of fol-de-rol in the following sayings:

"Blow out the candle and if the wick smoulders a long time, look out for bad weather." (Doubtful.)

"When the camphor in the bottle is 'riley' a storm is brewing." (Good rule.)

"If the sun sets in a cloud look out for rain next day." (Good rule).

"When one's joints ache and old hurts pain anew, look out for rainy weather." (Good rule).

"From twelve till two
Tells what the day will do."

is a very accurate statement as is also

"If it rain before seven
It will drip before eleven." (Often true.)

and the one from Pike County, Pennsylvania,

"When the fog goes up a-hopping
The rain will come down a-dropping." (Often true.)

It was the habit of our own ancestors, and is of the savages and peasantry of to-day, to look with awe and fear upon any unusual appearance of the sky.

Old sailormen and weather-wise people do the same, for they have learned that unusual conditions of the sky often foretell unusual conditions of the weather and that the color of the sky affords a surprisingly good guide to the weather conditions for the coming day.

As an art student the writer spent one whole season making notes of the color schemes of the sunsets and in so doing made an interesting discovery which is that all sunset colors are the same as those of the rainbow and arranged in the same order. Altho one might suppose in viewing a sunset that there was no system in the arrangement of colors, it is because the light reflected on the clouds apparently breaks the order of the rainbow.

It was after the author had made his discovery of the arrangement of the colors that the terrible volcanic eruption at Java occurred which sent a tidal wave around the earth and filled the atmosphere with an impalpable volcanic dust that remained suspended in the air for a whole season. During that season we had many cloudless sunsets, but the fine dust suspended in the air reflected the prismatic colors and confirmed the author's analysis, for the sky then appeared decked in rainbow colors and arranged in the order that they are in a rainbow.

Another thing that the author discovered on his sketching excursions, was, that the red of the sunset sky has a decided tendency to vermillion in color whereas the red in the sky of sunrise is of a more rosy color, and is what might be called a pink sky.

"The sun reveals the secrets of the sky,
And who dares give the source of light the lie?"

Not only does a red sunset foretell fine weather and a ruddy sunrise bad weather, but there are other tints which speak with equal clearness and accuracy. A.bright yellow sky in the morning indicates wind; a pale yellow foretells rain. A more intense yellow often occurs in the late afternoon when the rain is between us and the western sun and it gives the whole scenery a charming bright color owing to the yellow light on the leaves and grass making the green lighter and brighter. This tells us that it will rain, is close by and we will see it in a few minutes.

If in the morning the sky is of a dull gray color, the indications for a good day may be considered favorable. Generally speaking, it may be said that any deep or unusual hue betokens either rain or wind in summer and blustering wind and snow squalls in winter.

> "Evening red and morning gray
> Will set the traveler on his way;
> But evening gray and morning red
> Will bring down rain upon his head."

or

> "The evening gray and morning red,
> Put on your hat or you'll wet your head."
> "When the sun sets in the clear
> An easterly wind you need not fear."

"The sun sets weeping in the lowly west, witness storms to come, woe, and unrest."

E. B. Dunn, exforecast official in charge of the United States Weather Bureau, New York City, is quoted as saying, "that a red sunrise means a wet day." The setting of the sun as a red mist of fire presages warmer weather on the morrow.

Should the day grow very warm, and towards evening

the clouds apparently rest on the western horizon, becoming grayish at the base, the wind dying away and the atmosphere unusually quiet, look out for a thunder storm.

> "Fog on the hill
> Brings water to the mill.
> Fog in the vale
> Catch it in a pail!"

The latter meaning that one pail would hold all the moisture to be found.

WET AND DRY MOON (UNRELIABLE)

The superstition of the wet and dry moon is current with the negroes and is said to have existed among the Indians of the Potomac basin. It is that the crescent floating on its back forebodes a dry month, because it is then said to hold water, but if tipped upon its end it will be wet, as the water then runs out. This belief in a wet and dry moon also exists in the New England States and the Middle West.

Sailors, of course, refer frequently to the barometer and find it convenient to express many important facts in rhymes, and a few of the more prominent are here given:

> "First rise, after low,
> Indicates a stronger blow."

Also,

> "Long foretold, long last,
> Short notice, soon past."

To which may be added:

> "In squalls,
> When the rain's before the wind,
> Halyards, sheets and braces, mind."

And:

> "When the wind's before the rain
> Soon you may make sail again."

Also, speaking generally:

> "When the glass falls low,
> Prepare for a blow;
> When it rises high
> Let all your kites fly."

WEATHER BUREAU WEATHER SIGNS

In the neighborhood of New York, the Weather Bureau gives the following signs: "When we have a south to southwest wind, for from half day to a day in spring, autumn and winter, we may expect rain.

"Our summer rain fall is preceded by southerly winds for one or two days, and the numerous local summer showers usually begin about the turn of the barometer from falling to rising.

"When storms come from the south or southwest, the rain or snow is preceded by east to northeast winds, precipitation quickly following the shift of the wind to the south or southwest.

"In all seasons, the highest winds generally come from the northwest with rising barometer.

"The warmest periods of spring and winter come when the wind is from the south, the warmest weather of summer and autumn occurs when the wind is from the southwest.

"We have our coldest weather in spring, autumn and winter when the wind is from the northwest; and the weather is coolest in summer when the winds are from the northwest, north or northeast."

Three foggy or misty mornings indicate rain. A rising

fog indicates fair weather, if the fog settles down expect rain.

Fog from the sea, look for fair weather. Fog from the land, look for rain in New England.

Hoarfrost indicates rain.

In California heavy frost brings heavy rain, no frost no rain. The larger the halo around the moon the nearer the rain clouds, and the sooner the rain may be expected.

CHAPTER XXVI

WEATHER SIGNS

Predictions from Animals, Birds, Fishes and Insects, Founded on Observation, Fancy, Superstition and Imagination

In the good old days, when the old ladies of the best families smoked corn-cob pipes or took snuff as they sat in the chimney corners and thumbed their almanacs to see what the weather conditions would be the following winter or spring, everybody believed in many weather signs which are now forgotten. To doubt the prophecy based on the breast bone of the goose, for instance, was to be a heretic and an outcast of society and one whose character was not above suspicion.

Superstitions

In the days of our great-grandparents, superstition and imagination played a delightfully important part in their lives; romance and poetry were more highly esteemed than in this day of horrid scientific wars and aeroplanes and submarines; everybody in the olden times more than half believed in witches and fairies and as for ghosts? Well, the person who had not seen one or two was a very unobserving personage indeed. So, of course, all sorts of funny weather signs were considered infallible, as indeed many of them are now in some rural districts and in all lumber camps.

The lumber boss in the north woods to-day is not too bigoted to consult the local goose-bone prophet before laying his plans for the winter work.

There can be no question but that things which affect the comfort of birds and beasts are always noted by them,

187

and things which do not affect their comfort are not heeded. All the birds, mammals and even insects seem to have brains enough to know the difference between friendliness and hostility.

Even in the days before they were protected by law, the animals of Yellowstone Park feared not the terror-inspiring, roaring and spouting of the hot springs; trout will not move when a train thunders over the bridge crossing their brook, because in both these instances the creatures have learned that these things do not harm them. So it is fair to suppose that birds and beasts note the approach of storms for the reason that the danger and discomfort of storms has impressed itself upon them. It is said, by the Highlanders, that the deer in Scotland quit the exposed mountain tops hours before the coming storm is noticed by man.

BIRDS AND STORMS

Flying high in the air the birds can see the whisps of cirrus clouds, also the big balloon-like mountains of cumulus clouds, or "thunder caps," also the dark roll of cotton-like clouds which fringes the edge of the onrushing thunder squall; or the ragged aërial tramps of the sky that trail their tattered garments across the horizon, foretelling strong winds, or that terrible black funnel-shaped cloud which unmistakably marks the awful death-dealing tornado.

All these things may be noted by the birds flying high overhead long before they are seen by the men creeping like ants, away down below on the earth surface.

"Clamorous as a parrot against the rain" said Shakespeare.

It is very probable that the birds not only see but recognize their enemies in the sky as quickly as they have learned

to distinguish them on earth.   When birds of long flight
hang around the home base they foretell a storm.

> "When the peacock loudly bawls
> Soon we'll have both rain and squalls."

The small bird does not live that does not know and
fear a hawk; all crows know when a man has a gun and keep
out of its reach, altho they may pay but small heed to an
unarmed man.   But while the birds of the upper air may
be able to note the approaching storm long before we poor
earth-bound mortals can discover it, yet this cannot be true
of our barnyard fowls; they must know of the approaching
storm by some other means than their sight (if they are
really conscious of it at all) either by their feeling of some
peculiar condition of the atmosphere, or by noting the action
of the flying birds overhead.

> "If the cock goes crowing to bed
> He'll certainly rise with a wet head."

When chickens pick up small pebbles and are noisier
than usual they foretell rain.   If cocks crow early and late
clapping their wings, rain is expected.   If fowls betake
themselves to the ash heap, sand bank or dusty road to
roll and flutter, rain is near; the same is true when they all
seem intent upon oiling their feathers.   Guinea-fowls give
forth their rasping cries, more than is common, before a
rain.

Every observer has sometime or other noted the sudden
silence of the birds preceding a serious storm.   At any rate
from the time when Eve tended the jungle fowls for Adam
in the Garden of Eden, certain actions of the fowls have
been believed to foretell weather; take as an instance the
petrels.   The stormy petrels derive their name from the

belief of sailors that when the petrels follow a vessel it is to warn the sailors of a coming tempest.

> "When the geese gang out to sea
> Good weather there will surely be."

GOOSE-BONE

In order to give the signs contained in the breastbone of a goose correctly, the writer has consulted a number of authorities, old weather prophets in farming districts, and such national authorities as the prophecies of Ezekiel Bonzy and his greater rival Elias Hartz, the veteran and almost centenarian goose-bone prophet of Pennsylvania, who foretold the weather each year for half a century and kept a collection of dried breastbones of geese representing a quarter of a century. Also, the writer has read the more modern prophet, John T. Timmons, whose forecasts of weather excite considerable interest among many people. From all of these great authorities he has formulated the following:

BLUE BONE RULES

About November the 20th, or on Thanksgiving Day, kill a goose, roast it, serve and carve it, being careful not to cut or deface the breastbone; carefully remove all the meat from the breast bone, dry the bone by hanging it on a nail over the door, then watch for the coloration which will develop. Blue, black or purple indicates cold weather, while white indicates mild weather. Purple tips to the bone foretell cold weather next spring. If the blue color branches out in lines towards the edge of the bone there will be open weather until New Year's Day. If the bone is blotched with blue and white, it tells us that the winter will be open and shut. But if the bone is broad and white an open winter may be expected.

If, however, the bone is dark colored or blue all over its surface, my! look out for a regular old-fashioned cold winter.

So many people believe in these signs that the writer will not endanger his popularity by calling them silly, but nevertheless he prefers the weather man at Washington to the best goose-bone prophet. For the fun of the thing three goose-bones were secured Thanksgiving Day, 1916; they are all white, the reader can himself tell how accurate was their prophecy.

"Everything is lovely and the goose hangs high" is probably a corruption of "everything is lovely when the goose honks high."

Until the last four or five years the migrating wild geese have each year flown over the writer's house in Flushing, awakening him by their honking, and in our calendar of Pioneer and Indian seasons we may see that the cold season is named from the call of the wild geese, showing that this bird's cry was the sign of winter among the Redmen. Wild geese flying by large bodies of water denote a change in the weather.

GOOSE-HONK SIGN OF COLD

As far back as the people of this generation can remember, the honk of the wild goose overhead has been accepted as the certain sign of an approaching cold snap in the fall and of the breaking up of winter in the spring.

Even the most unobserving persons have noted that migratory birds fly south before cold and stormy weather and north prior to warm weather, but only the Indians seem to have noticed that before the approach of dangerous winds, cyclones and tornadoes migratory birds fly in circles or restlessly about and exhibit a nervous state of indecision. This (1917) October while camping far north of Lake Superior the author saw and heard many geese flying overhead; there were thousands of them, and after them came a cold wave and a driving snow storm.

CROWS AND RAIN

Crows fly low cawing loudly and wheel in great circles before a rain, but when they fly high in pairs it denotes fair weather. Also lone crows flying heavily overhead emitting occasional doleful quokes! is considered by hunters as a rain sign.

SEA-GULLS

Gulls will fly high and circle around, uttering sharp cries before a storm. Flying high over the land is a sign of an approaching storm; the same birds congregated in numbers on the salt meadows and inland bays tell the sailor that there is a storm at sea. But pigeons make no long flight just before a rain. Herons become uneasy before rain and will fly aimlessly about.

THE USUALLY SILENT CUCKOO

Can be heard clucking in the trees in anticipation of the coming shower, while the robin perches himself on the highest branch and sings loud and joyfully at the approach of rain.

BARNYARD FOWLS

That domestic poultry molt early before a cold winter and late before a mild one needs proof. So also does the statement that when wild ducks and wild geese shed their feathers early there will be a cold winter. Fowls also are said to develop thicker coats of down and feather for a cold winter, but this is not accepted by cold-blooded scientists.

DUCKS QUACKING

Ducks quacking a great deal foretell rain. Roosters crowing in the rain are calling upon it to stop and the rain is said to obey the roosters command. But roosters crowing at night foretell rain for the morrow. When ducks and geese spend considerable time oiling their feathers look for rain.

RUFFED GROUSE

strut on the old drumming logs and beat their drum at night before a snow storm. Cranes are restless, often screaming and making uncouth noises before a rain. The great horned owl and the barred owl hoot continuously for more than their usual periods before a rain or snow storm. When the field sparrows splash around flapping their wings in the puddles, while the woodpeckers which are usually so silent, cry "yoo, yoo, yoo, yoo," it is because rain is coming.

The author does not pretend to separate by a definite line the folk lore and superstitions from the reliable signs as noted in this section of the bird signs; but he does contend that the approaching storm does affect the action of animals and this is not doubted by any woodsman, hunter, or fisherman.

THE BULL-FROG

It is well known that the bull-frog changes color at pleasure but it may not be as well known that when he is light green or yellow it means fair weather, when he is dark green or almost black it means foul weather; the writer is one who does not know this to be true.

FISH WEATHER SIGNS

Frequently the author has had occasion to note the unusual activity of fish during the approach of a thunder storm, and while he has had no particular luck during a downpour of rain, he has caught his largest fish just before the breaking of a storm; this has happened too often to be a mere coincidence.

In truth bass seem to bite most recklessly when the lightning is cracking overhead, much too near to the fisherman for personal comfort; this usually happens during that short period which sometimes precedes a sudden downpour of rain in the summer time.

"When the wind is in the east
Then they bite the very least,
When the wind is in the west
Then they bite the very best,
When the wind is in the south
It blows the bait in the fish's mouth."

thus saith the old verse, but this does not agree with the writer's personal experience. Mr. James W. Johnson, of Binghamton, and the author have for several seasons kept a careful record of their catches of big fish, noting the kind of weather, direction of wind, bait and manner of fishing, and after a careful review of the notes they found that the direction of the wind has apparently no influence on the action of the small-mouthed bass.

In the inland lakes of Pike County, Pennsylvania, the fish are disinclined to bite between 10 A.M. and 4 P.M. unless the sky is overcast. This is apparently because they do not like the direct rays of the sun; but the direction of the wind does not seem to affect them one way or the other.

During the prevalence of great forest fires when the air is heavy with smoke, the bass seem to lack energy and ambition, and altho they rise to the bait they only lazily mouth it and then leave it without taking hold.

Heat and cold, light and dark, undoubtedly affect the fish, as does also the close proximity of a storm. Just after a rain the fish in the ponds do not bite freely; this is probably owing to the fact that the rain has washed a plentiful supply of food into the water. "When pike rest quietly on the bottom look for rain." Immediately before rain both salt and fresh water fish are more playful and eager to bite. The appearance of great numbers of fish on the west coast of the Gulf of Mexico is a sign of easterly winds and foul weather.

It is said that easterly winds are good for sea bass fishing, but the writer is a fresh-water fisherman and knows little of this from personal experience at sea. During one of his few salt-water fishing trips, however, he discovered that all the very big blue fish were to be found in the shade of the masses of floating seaweed. The day was exceedingly hot and the fish apparently sought the shade as do the cattle in a pasture.

"The sun at its meridian height
Illumined the depth of the sea,
And the fishes beginning to sweat,
Cried, 'Darn it, how hot we shall be.' "

Bubbles in the water over a clam bed appear before rain.

Old salt water fisherman aver that the fish seek the deep water on hot days, because it is cooler and that they seek the deep water in winter because it is warmer than the shallow water, this also is the case in fresh water lakes. Old salts claim that on hot days the fish are off shore or loafing around the rocks in the shade of marine plants where they make themselves as comfortable as the hot weather will permit. Trout jump before a rain and the schools of herrings swim faster.

FISH FORETELL COLD WEATHER

The salt-water fisherman also declares that the fish know in advance what the weather is to be; in winter it is said that the fish will make for deep water hours or maybe as much as a day before a cold snap arrives.

If the flounders are absent from their usual haunts, it indicates cold weather is approaching. But if flounders are found in their usual haunts, altho that particular day may be very cold, their presence foretells a warm spell approaching.

INSECT WEATHER SIGNS, RELIABLE AND OTHERWISE

It is claimed that if you count the number of chirrups a cricket makes in a minute and subtract it from the number of degrees marked by the thermometer the remainder will give you a number by which you can always tell the temperature.

Thus, suppose the cricket chirrups forty times in a minute and the mercury at the same time stands at seventy degrees, the forty from seventy leaves thirty. Now then, the next time the cricket pipes up and you count, maybe seventy chirrups to the minute, seventy plus thirty equal one hundred degrees.

This is interesting even if not reliable, and apparently does show that the hotter the weather the faster the cricket plays his fiddle, which at least agrees with probability, for we know that in very cool weather all insects are sluggish.

LOCUST CICADA, OR HARVEST FLY

The locust singing at dawn on a summer morning is said to be calling "Heat! heat! heat!"

HOUSE FLIES

When flies alight on bald heads, insist upon tickling one's nose, creep brazenly over one's hands, it is a certain sign of rain, as all good grandmothers will aver. When flies congregate in swarms they feel that rain is approaching.

GNATS

Gnats dance in clouds before one's face, moving along ahead of the pedestrians on the open road telling him to expect fair weather.

EARTH WORMS

Plentiful marks of earthworms, that is, little bunches of leaves gathered in small heaps over the lawn by these worms, foretell a change in the weather.

ANTS

Ants on low ground migrate before a "cloud burst." When ants are busy piling up pallets of earth around their holes look for fair weather, but look for storms when ants travel in lines, Indian style. If, however, the ants travel in scattering formation it indicates fair weather.

CATERPILLARS

Some people claim to foretell mild or severe winters by the markings on caterpillars, but just how this is done has never been explained to the writer.

BEES AND HORNETS

A bee needs no umbrella, he is said to be never caught in a shower. When bees in the autumn are busy feeding on the necter to be found in the open it is claimed that they are then saving their stored honey for food for the coming long and severe winter. But if these insects are discovered eating honey in their hives it is because there will be an open winter and no scarcity of food.

> "When bees to distance wing their flight
> Days are warm and skies are bright,
> But when their flight ends near at home
> Stormy weather is sure to come."

When hornets build their paper nest in the bushes near the ground or on the low branches of the trees it signifies a warm winter—maybe.

GRASSHOPPERS, KATYDIDS AND CRICKETS

When the katydids sing late in the fall and the crickets continue to chirrup long after their usual quitting time, and when grasshoppers are still abundant late in the autumn, it is said to be a certain sign of a mild winter. It is true that there has been no cold weather that season to kill them, whatever may happen later.

SPIDERS

When the spider webs are beaded with dew in the morning, each thread appearing like a string of diamonds, it indicates fair weather, so the housewives say; lazy, indolent spiders foretell rain.

The big yellow and black garden spider that makes the beautiful polygon webs with zig-zag stairways up their centres, also the small garden spiders which make similar webs, minus the zig-zag stairways, are all said to spin short and thick lines before rain and long and thin lines before fair weather. No matter how bad the weather may be it may be safely inferred that it will soon change to fair weather when the spiders are observed repairing their webs, so say the good wives.

MAMMAL WEATHER SIGNS

These signs are mostly directly descended from magic and witchcraft and are not very reliable, altho they are entertaining.

Every country boy will tell you that the muskrat knows ahead of time what the winter is to be. If there is to be little snow and a dry spring the muskrats will build small houses

out in the water, but if there is to be much snow and conse-
quent floods in the spring the muskrats will build their
houses much higher up on the banks of the creek and ponds,
to prevent them from being submerged and washed away
by the spring floods.

A CAT'S TAIL AS A BAROMETER

Some authorities claim that there are from 11,000 to
13,000 hairs in a cat's tail, and the writer would much rather
accept these figures as being true than to try to verify them
by counting the hairs; but the reader may count the hairs
in a cat's tail, and if he finds about 11,000 he may look for
a mild winter, but if there are on or about 13,000 it is time
to go buy himself a warm fur overcoat, for he will need
such a coat before spring—maybe.

The cat washing its face on the door-step foretells rain.
All fur-bearing animals are supposed to wear heavier coats
of fur on the approach of a severe winter than they do prior
to a mild season; trapper and fur dealers believe this to be
true.

SQUIRRELS

It is said that squirrels build their nests carelessly before
a mild winter, but carefully before a cold one—The squirrels'
nest is in a hollow tree in winter, but it seems that the summer
nest of leaves is referred to. Also if the squirrels and wild
mice lay up a big supply of nuts, that, hunters will tell you,
foretells a cold winter.

BATS

It is true that the bats fly high in search of insects when
the weather is to be fair and low before a rain. This is because the insects are affected by the condition of the atmosphere and fly high in the light atmosphere which precedes
fair weather.

PORPOISES

Porpoises come north and whales are supposed to migrate too on the approach of warm weather and, like the swallows, the appearance of these air-breathing sea mammals along the coast is looked upon as a sign of spring.

HOGS

Porpoises are sometimes called "sea hogs" but sea hogs are not the only hogs gifted with prophecy. The writer well remembers seeing the pigs in the streets of Cincinnati and comparatively recently in the streets of Long Island City where they ran at large, and to have noticed them upon various occasions running around with chips or sticks or cobs in their mouths. When a pig cuts up antics with a cob in its mouth there is to be a change of weather, a storm or cold snap, so said my grandmother, and she had had almost ninety years of observation to back her judgment.

CATTLE

Before a storm cattle will often gather at one end of the pasture with their tails to the windward. When the cattle lie down immediately, or soon after they are turned out in the pasture, it is not because they are tired but because they want to let you know that it is going to rain. Also when cattle sniff the air and paw the earth, like ill-tempered buffalo bulls, it is a sign of rain. All shepherds aver that when their flocks are unusually playful, leaping and butting, there is a storm in sight. Horses and cattle stretch their necks and sniff the air that smells of a coming storm. Horses will shy at a stick or a paper and are more than usually restless before a storm.

GROUNDHOG DAY

Groundhog Day has become a regular institution and its advent is noted by all the newspapers throughout the land. Of course, we know the groundhog's sign to be but a bit of superstition or folk lore and not reliable as are some of the preceding signs, but it is a weather sign all the same, and as such must be recorded. The 2nd of February is the day when the ground hog wakes up from its long winter's nap, and comes forth from its hole to look around and see how the spring is progressing. If it sees its shadow, it forthwith returns to its lair, for it knows that the backbone of winter is not yet broken. But if the day is cloudy the groundhog will not see its shadow and the woodchuck and all good housewives will know that spring is nigh.

OPPOSSUM

Some people pretend to prophesy from the condition of the milts of the oppossum. The milts are the spleen, and when they are thin at what might be termed the "autumn" ends and thicken abruptly and continues thick for a space then gradually taper to the "spring" end, the weather in January and February will be very severe.

A wilderness hunter can tell by the weather whether to hunt for the bears on the hillsides among the beech trees or down in the swails. The same knowledge is true of wing shots with the birds, these men will tell you when to find the ruffed grouse in the swails or on the uplands, and when the fall flight of woodcocks is on, the gunners know by the kind of day just where to look for the birds.

This bird knowledge is true of the geese and duck hunter also. But! these last instances are all relating to times when the creatures adapt their action to *existing conditions* of the weather, not to what the weather is *going to be.*

SNAKES, TOADS AND FROGS

It is an old and popular superstition that to kill a snake or a frog will produce rain! One reason for this is possibly that in excessive dry seasons all sorts of frogs and reptiles are very scarce, because all such creatures are seeking the moist places, consequently if you meet one, whether you kill it or not it possibly means that the atmosphere indicates rain. Before a mild winter snakes are very slow in "denning up" that is in seeking the crevass cave, or rock ledge, where they spend their winter.

Of course the reader knows that the tree toads sing loudly before rain, but we must not forget that there are thousands of people who do not know a tree toad's voice when they hear it.

One of the most ancient weather signs is found in the horse; when Dobbins sheds his hair freely the winter will be mild, because the horse will not then need a heavy coat as protection from the elements.

Many farmers pretend to foretell the weather by observing the actions of Molly Cottontail; if the rabbits sit up erect like little posts that means there will be little cold weather.

PLANTS AS WEATHER SIGNS

Tree trunks appear to be darker before a storm. Sensitive plants contract their leaves and blossoms on the approach of rain. When moss is soft and damp expect rain, when it is dry and brittle expect clear weather. The author has seen it so dry in northern Canada that one's footprints in it were as distinct as if it were snow in place of moss. Preceding rain the silver poplar, cotton wood and quaking aspen trees show the underside of their leaves. Sycamore, lime and plane trees when trembling in the wind show the under surface of their leaves too.

The morning-glories close their blossoms on the approach of rain. Clover leaves close up and display their underside, and pink-eyed pimpernel closes in the daytime before a rain. In the swamps the carnivorous pitcher plants open their mouths before a rain.

If the fruit buds are large look for a cold winter.

At corn-husking time when the boys and girls are seeking for the red ears which entitles the lucky finder to a kiss, it is often remarked by the old folks that the husks are very much thicker than usual and fit snugly to the ear; then the wise ones say, "Um, um! it's going to be a cold winter and we must lay in plenty of cord wood." Or the husks may be few, thin and loose on the ears of corn and the wise ones will say, "Ah! a mild winter is ahead of us." But the young folks are more interested in their search for the red ear than in what sort of winter is to come, and when a lad finds such an ear and claims the privilege that the red ears bestow, all is sunshine to him even though the sky be overcast.

NUTS

Chestnuts, hickory-nuts, walnuts and all kind of nuts are supposed to have thin shells to indicate a "soft" winter and hard shells to indicate a "hard" winter. Of course it is here necessary to explain to our provincial New England neighbor that walnuts are what is known to them as *black walnuts* and what they insist upon calling *walnuts* are hickory-nuts, thus confusing the stranger within their gates.

Deep snow will not be coming if the wheat does not grow high. If the chaff that covers many seeds is light, look out for a mild season. Heavy fall pasture indicates a mild winter say some folks.

Each town and village has its local weather prophets, and this is particularly noticeable among the Pennsylvania

"Dutch." These good folks claim that the early falling of leaves from the apple tree indicates a mild winter, so also does the scarcity of acorns, but when the persimmon trees are loaded with fruit it foretells very cold weather.

If the bark on young trees is very thin, look for a mild winter. This gives the trees a foresight into the future which belongs to two-legged nature fakirs; but we all love the marvellous and like to believe things that common sense tells us are not true, hence we have mixed up the scientific signs with superstition, so that it is difficult to separate the really reliable ones from the folk-lore fairy story products. For instance, the following verse must not be taken seriously:

> "St. Swithin's Day, if then dost rain,
> For forty days it will remain.
> St. Swithin's Day, if then be fair,
> For forty days will rain nae mair."

But this collection from an old Irish reader contains many signs which are quite reliable.

> "The hollow winds begin to blow,
> The clouds look black, the glass is low;
> The soot falls down, the spaniels sleep,
> And spiders from their cobwebs creep.
> Last night the sun went pale to bed,
> The moon in halos hid her head.
> The boding shepherd heaves a sigh,
> For, see, a rainbow spans the sky;
> The walls are damp, the ditches small,
> Closed is the pink-eyed pimpernel.
> Hark! How the chairs and tables crack:
> Old Betty's joints are on the rack;
> Loud quack the ducks, the peacocks cry;

The distant hills are looking nigh.
How restless are the snorting swine!
The busy flies disturb the kine;
Low o'er the grass the swallow wings,
The cricket, too, how sharp he sings.
Puss on the hearth, with velvet paws,
Sits wiping o'er her whiskered jaws.
Through the clear stream the fishes rise
And nimbly catch the incautious flies.
The glow worms, numerous and bright,
Illumed the dewy dell last night.
At dusk the squalled toad was seen,
Hopping and crawling o'er the green;
The whirling wind the dust obeys,
And in the rapid eddy plays;
The frog has changed his yellow vest,
And in a russet coat is dressed.
Though June the air is cold and chill,
The mellow blackbird's voice is shrill;
My dog, so altered in his taste,
Quits mutton bones, on grass to feast.
And see yon rooks, how odd their flight.
They imitate the gliding kite,
And headlong downward seem to fall
As if they felt the piercing ball.
Twill surely rain, I see with sorrow
Our jaunt must be put off to-morrow.'"

CHAPTER XXVII
FLAGS—THE RED, WHITE AND BLUE

THE ORIFLAMME, BANNERETS AND BANNERS, TREES, RATTLESNAKES, AND MOTTOES ON EARLY AMERICAN FLAGS; EVIDENT ORIGIN OF THE STARS AND STRIPES; THE RED CROSS OF ST. GEORGE; THE CROSS OF ST. ANDREW; BETSY ROSS; THE GRAND UNION FLAG; BIRTH OF THE FLAG OF THE UNITED STATES

WHEN you again sing "Three Cheers for the Red, White and Blue!" remember that these are probably the most ancient of all flag colors.

In the first place be it remembered that the red, white and blue are the colors of the ancient Jewish Church, and that the cloth on the table before the ark of the covenant was red, white, and blue.

Also, do not forget that over a thousand years ago a seven-foot giant with a sheep-skin robe, known as the Emperor Charlemagne, had a red, white, and blue tassel on his oriflamme—well what is an oriflamme?—a sort of banderole, and a banderole is?—a kind of ornamented streamer or pennon attached to a lance near the spear head; a pennant was called a pennon.

BANNERETS

In the olden times, as far back as Edward the first of England, when a bachelor had long followed the wars and could report with fifty men-at-arms, all the archers and cross-bow men appertaining to them, he also was wont to bring his private or personal pennon and with it a request for leave to bear a *banner*, this granted the king's lieutenant would then cut the tail off the streamer and thus leave a square piece of cloth called a banner, which was a sign, signal, or symbol announcing that the bachelor was now a

206

mighty captain with the title of banneret.   Just before
the battle of Nafars, one, John G. Haundos, petitioned the
Black Prince and Don Pedro, King of Castile, to be made
a banneret.

L'Ame De L'Oriflamme

After the revolution in 1789, when France adopted the
tricolor she was harkening away back to that great big
roughneck Charlemagne. The red, white, and blue inspired
the mighty warriors of France in the ninth century and
sent them singing to battle, and when William the Con-
querer conquered England he bore an oriflamme which was
a duplicate of that of Charlemagne.

The oriflamme went through the crusade and faced
the great Saladin. When the red, white and blue reached
Palestine it had but returned to its original home, the home
of the Old Jewish Church.

It is extremely doubtful that any of our Colonial forefathers ever took the trouble to trace the red, white and
blue back to the crusaders, to William the Conqueror, Charlemagne or the Jewish Church; they did not have to do this
in order to find our national colors, for Great Britain still
retained them in her banner and it was only necessary to
rearrange the designs in order to make a new flag and then
the red, white and blue were ours too!

During the war of the States in 1861, all the Union people
near the border wore proudly on their left breasts a red,
white and blue cockade while the Confederates just as
proudly sported red, white and red cockades now we *all*
stick to the glorious red, white and blue.

Flag Trees

The pine, elm and palmetto trees are intimately associated with American history, and the pictures of one

or the other often appear upon our early coin and flags. The palmetto tree when used on a flag usually has a blue field, naturally these latter banners originated in the South, usually in South Carolina, that being called the Palmetto State, although the traveller thru that State seldom sees live palmetto trees growing anywhere except in tubs after the manner Southern plants are grown in the North. There is, or was, in front of the Capitol grounds a very beautiful iron palmetto, planted and camouflaged to represent a live plant.

At the corner of Washington and Essex Streets, in Boston, once stood the famous Liberty Tree, and under its spreading branches many partiotic meetings were held, and there protests were made against the infamous Stamp Act.

The Canadians are a tea-drinking nation, the Americans are a coffee-drinking nation, and the reason of this is that a foolish English King, Parliament and House of Lords, paid no attention to the protest of the Americans against the Stamp Act, and this so angered the Americans that on December the 6th, 1775, they threw all the tea from the ships over-board into the harbor.

EFFECTS OF TEA ON AMERICANS

After that anyone drinking tea in America was suspected of disloyalty to the American cause, and our country thereafter became a coffee-drinking nation. This is an interesting bi-product of the Stamp Act, the important thing is, that the silly German-like attempt to enforce the Stamp Act gave birth to a new flag; caused Great Britain to loose her most valuable colony, and caused us to build a great nation to join England in a supreme effort to defend that Democracy which she denied us a long time ago.

For years the red cross of St. George on a white ground was England's Union Jack, but in 1606 when Scotland was adopted as part of Great Britain the white field of the Union Jack, evidently was not the proper background for a white cross, therefore it was changed to blue and over it was emblazoned the upright red cross of St. George and the diagonal white cross of the Scotch St. Andrew. This was the flag carried by the Mayflower when she came to anchor at Plymouth, and the Constant when she sailed for Jamestown.

Thus you see that when our gallant British cousins speak of their flag as one that has "braved a thousand years in battle and in breeze" they are using poetic license, and when they do so they forget that the Union Jack up in the northwest corner of the flag, as it appears to-day, was not born until 1801, but thank Providence old England herself has braved a thousand years in battle and we hope may live in peace for a thousand years longer.

The truth is the American Flag is one of the oldest flags, altho our country is one of the youngest nations.

The French flag of three perpendicular red, white, and blue stripes was born in 1794; the Spanish flag in 1785; while the Italian and German flags are only as old as the present form of Empire and Kingdom they represent.

The American flag, as we know it to-day, was born in the year 1777, and it consists now, as it did then, of thirteen red and white stripes with a constellation of stars on a blue ground in the northwest corner of the flag. Our first flag has the thirteen stars arranged in a circle, to-day all our smaller flags have but thirteen stars also arranged in a circle the same as the flag of 1777; but in our big flags we arranged the stars in rows, one star for each State in the Union.

Stars and Stripes

Anyone looking over the flags of Great Britain may see where we found our thirteen red and white stripes, but from whence the stars?

A flag was needed to represent the new country, and all sorts of experiments were made producing a lot of freak flags, pine tree flags rattlesnake flags, but none of these were satisfactory and all of them were eventually abandoned; they lacked dignity and were too local and explicit in their picturegraphs, many were more appropriate as political cartoons than as national flags.

Pine trees are not characteristic of some parts of the country and palmetto trees do not grow in Maine or New England. The rattlesnake, however, is really characteristic of United States, and was a great favorite among our Revolutionary ancestors as an emblem. First, because it is typical of this country and found nowhere else; second, because its bright lidless eyes are a symbol of vigilance; third, because by putting thirteen rattles on its tail they could represent the thirteen states. It was claimed that one rattle alone could make no noise but that thirteen of them singing together would make the stoutest heart flutter. The old motto on the rattlesnake flags:

"don't tread on me"

was certainly fraught with meaning, nevertheless; it does not make a noble symbol, and furthermore flags with people, saints, snakes, crowns, and eagles flavor too strongly of the Old World.

What we wanted was a brand new design to fit a brand new country. Now then, there was a flag recognized and protected by England, used by the East India Company;

a company chartered by Queen Elizabeth in 1600; it was a flag familiar to the whole world and depicted in the books and encyclopedias as early as 1759 as the English flag. This flag had thirteen red and white stripes and for a Union Jack had the red cross of St. George on a white field, Fig. 328. It is claimed that Benjamin Franklin wanted the United States to adopt this flag, and it is admitted that the flag was familiar to all seafaring people.

When the white cross of St. Andrew was added in 1606 to the red cross of St. George on the British flag, the British were confronted with the problem of placing a white cross on a white ground, which they sidestepped by adopting a blue ground upon which to put the white cross and the red cross of St. George over it, and this, Fig. 328½, was our first national flag; that is, the English Union Jack with the thirteen red and white stripes of the Old East India Company.

There can be no doubt of the source from whence we derive the suggestion of the thirteen red and white stripes: they helped make a banner which every artist recognized as possessing more life than any banner that floats. The reason of it is this: the waving of the flag gives an apparent separate motion to each of the thirteen stripes and causes the stars really to twinkle, which gives an appearance of real life and independent movement to the banner, not to be obtained with any other design.

A flag with one star and stripe has not the same effect; a flag with crosses or upright stripes, or coats-of-arms, make beautiful stationary decorations, but waving in the breeze they could never have inspired Key to compose the "Star Spangled Banner" or a similar ode, it was the twinkling of the stars, and the apparent separate motion of each stripe which gave inspiration to the poet. Of course, back of all that were the grand principles which our flag represents, principles which should appeal to the heart of every real man, and does appeal to the heart of every American boy.

When we come to the origin of the stars, which are now used on the blue ground, in place of the crosses, the subject is open to discussion.

ORIGIN OF THE STARS

Nothing in this world is created from nothing, everything grows from something else, that is, it is suggested or evolved from something else. You see, at first we owed our allegiance to England, and although we lived in America we were under the English King. We were slow in throwing off the yoke, and when we did at last break away, we discarded the crosses of St. George and St. Andrew.

Our old ancestors had no particular love for a cross on their banner, they were prejudiced; they had been carrying a cross on their backs so long that when they made up their minds to throw it off they also threw the crosses off their flag.

With the crosses removed this would leave a flag of thirteen red and white stripes with a blank blue Union Jack, and the problem was to find some other symbols to put on the blue field. Fortunately, George Washington's coat-of-arms had stripes and also some ornaments in the form of rowels from the spurs of knights; the rowel you know is a little pointed wheel on the spur with which the horseman touches up his steed to make him feel spry.

In heraldry these wheels are called pierced mullets, and on Washington's old coat-of-arms they were represented with holes in their centres, thus showing their origin. The Americans did not want anything which savored of royalty, monarchy or inherited titles on their banner, but these pierce mullets on Washington's coat-of-arms were really

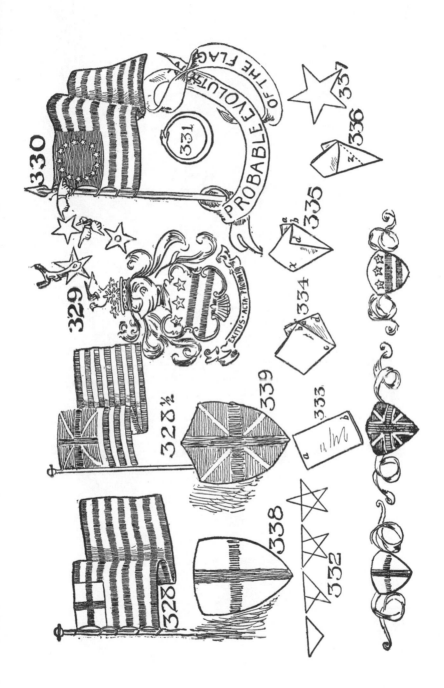

328

328½

329

330

331

331

PROBABLE EVOLUTION OF THE FLAG

332

333

334

335

336

338

339

in the form of five pointed stars. That suggested something big, for stars stand for LIGHT! And from the spur wheels, there can be little doubt, we derived the stars that sparkle and twinkle on our banner, "and wherever this flag comes and men behold it they see the symbols of light, it is the banner of Dawn!"

If the stripes on the flag, Fig. 328, did not remind George Washington and others of the stripes on the Washington shield, Fig. 329, then George and the others lacked imagination. The stripes were on the flag and the stripes were on his coat-of-arms. The cross was on the flag and we did not want it, there were star-like objects on the coat-of-arms, Fig.329, and by leaving out the hole in the centre they were five-pointed stars, Fig. 330, no other nation boasted a similar design. If this is not the way those old fellows reasoned, then their heads were more boney than history would lead us to believe.

It was Washington who abandoned the name of mullets, ignoring their origin but preserving their shape and the idea suggested by it, he said, "We take the star from Heaven, the red from our mother country, separating it by white stripes, thus showing that we have separated from her, and the white stripes shall go down to posterity, reppresenting liberty."

THE MEANING OF THE CIRCLE

A serpent with its tail in its mouth, (Fig. 331) makes a circle, the universal emblem of eternity—never ending, without end—and following this idea our forefathers put the thirteen stars in a circle, as they are at the present time in our small flags.

BETSY ROSS

Notwithstanding the pretty fable about Betsy Ross, showing the committee how to cut out the five pointed star with one clip of the scissors, we are compelled to believe that the mullets on Washington's coat-of-arms had more to do with the suggestion of stars for our flag. If the reader will look in the book, Jack-of-All Trades, by the author, on Page 220, he will see how to cut a six-pointed star with one clip of the scissors with at least as much ease as one can cut a five-pointed star.

THE GRAND UNION FLAG

Fig. 328½ cannot be anything but the child of Fig. 328. You will note in the diagram (Fig. 328½) that there are two crosses, the upright red cross of St. George and the X-shaped white cross of St. Andrew. These two crosses were combined in 1707; it was nearly a hundred years afterward that the red cross of St. Patrick found its place on the same flag, which was after the Irish Parliament had united with the British Parliament.

The author is afraid that in going over this history, he has been talking as if he was talking to men in place of young people, but he knows the boys will always forgive him when he mistakes them for *men*. The truth of the matter is that it has been men who have mixed us all up on this flag business and the author was unconsciously answering them in his talk. Of course we know that the men, the author included, are not near as bright as boys. However that may be, it was England that gave the East India Company the red and white striped flag, Fig. 328; but when by a stroke of genius or inspiration, the founders of this republic combined the stars on a blue ground with the thirteen red and white stripes they produced a flag which in itself was unique, and did not resemble any of the Old World standards. Henry Ward Beecher called it the flag of light, the flag of dawn, and such it is; it heralded the dawn of human rights, and as President Wilson has said, "It is the emblem of our unity, our power, our thought and purpose as a nation. It has no other character than that which we give it from generation to generation."

In other words, boys, that flag is a reflection of your own soul, it means great things and wonderful things, because YOU mean great things and wonderful things. If it is the "ugliest flag on earth" as one alien said of it, it is because the man who gave expression to such a thought had in his soul the ugliest *thoughts* on earth, for our flag is a magical mirror which reflects the images of the thoughts of those who behold it.

TREATY OF PEACE AND 1783

The treaty of peace between England and the United States was signed at Paris on September the third, 1783. This was an acknowledgment by Great Britain of the right of America to govern herself. The other nations stood by and consented to have us cut loose from our mother's apron strings. From this date the American Flag stood on equal grounds with the flags of other nations.

CHAPTER XXVIII

FOLLOWING THE CHANGES IN THE FLAG

From the Grand Union Standard to the Star Spangled Banner and Old Glory. The Stafford Flag; Paul Jones Flag, Five-, Six- and Eight-pointed Stars; The Easton Flag; Tragic Fate of Old Glory; Rules of Etiquette of the Flag

Betsy Ross Story Doubtful

We do not doubt that Betsy Ross made a flag, neither do we see any reason to doubt that she cut the stars out in the manner shown by Figs. 333-337, but we see no reason for giving her credit for designing the flag, or even the stars thereof.

It is claimed that the thirteen stripes on our flag were adopted to represent the thirteen States, there is little doubt that this was suggested to the minds of the designers of the flag, after they had discovered that the thirteen stripes on the East India Company's flag corresponded in number with the thirteen States, and this is in a measure confirmed by the fact that the

Stafford Flag

is apparently the first flag upon which the stars were used on the union blue field. It is a badly proportioned flag with but twelve stars, although it has the thirteen red and white stripes of the old East India Company flag. This flag was made by the Misses Mary and Sarah Austin, of Philadelphia, under the direction of a Mr. John Brown before the convention on February 5th, 1777, when Georgia took its place among the independent States of the Union, consequently there were only twelve states in the Union, hence the twelve stars. Apparently the Stafford flag is the first

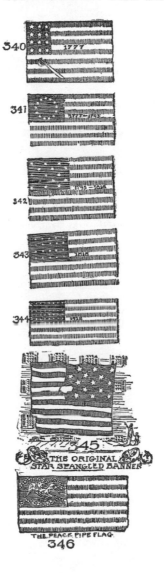

upon which a constellation of stars was used on the blue field of the Union Jack, Fig. 340. It is also claimed that the five-pointed stars on this flag were put there in compliance with the personally expressed wishes of George Washington himself.

The family legend regarding this flag conflicts with Paul Jones' statement in his journal. Both Stafford and Jones agree that a flag was shot from the mast of the Bon Homme Richard; Jones said that it was rescued, Stafford claimed that he is the one who jumped overboard and rescued it; both said that it was again put in place. Stafford said he nailed it to the mast, Jones said it went down with the ship. Stafford's heirs exhibit the flag, Fig. 340, with the nail holes still in it as the flag of the Bon Homme Richard.

The history of the Stafford flag is probably true except that it was not the one on the Bon Homme Richard, for all Americans love the memory of Paul Jones and must take his own words for it when he says that "the very last vestige mortal eyes ever saw of the Bon Homme Richard was the defiant waving of her unconquered and unstricken flag as she went down."

The Paul Jones Flag according to a circumstantial account of it in a footnote in Buell's "Life of Paul Jones," was made by a quilting party of girl admirers of the gallant Jones, among those present there was Helen Seavey, who was married in May, 1777, and donated her wedding gown for the "*thirteen*" white stars, Mary Langdon, Caroline Chandler and Augusta Pierce.

This flag was the first, and so far the only flag, that ever went down on the victorious ship which captured the ship that sunk it! and my readers join me I know in the desire to believe that the old flag still flies over the Bon Homme Richard, "the only ship ever sunk in victory."

THE GRAND UNION FLAG

Fig. 328½, claimed by Lieutenant-Commander Bryon McCandless and Gilbert Grosvenor, editor of the Geographical Magazine, to be the flag hoisted by Paul Jones on December 3rd, 1775, which is two years before the quilting party of the dear Continental girls who made Paul a flag.

This flag had the British Union Jack in the upper left-hand corner in place of the stars, Fig. 328½. Regarding this or some other flag Paul Jones wrote to Honorable Robert Morris as follows: "It was my fortune as senior officer of the first Lieutenants to hoist myself the flag of America." The Grand Union Flag appears first in print on the North Carolina paper scrip money, April 2nd, 1776. At Cambridge, Mass., a similar flag was hoisted in May, 1776. This flag design is known as the Grand Union Flag.

ADDITIONAL STRIPES

Although it was resolved on June 14th, 1777, that the flag of the thirteen States be alternate red and white stripes, that the union be thirteen stars, white with a blue field, representing the new constellation, our flag was still to change, and it began by adding stripes, as well as stars, for each new state, until, 1818, when we had a flag of fifteen stars and fifteen stripes, Fig. 342, and this brings us to the Star Spangled Banner, for it was a flag of this description which inspired Key to write our national anthem.

Our trim, well-proportioned flag was becoming awkward and stubby, and if we had continued to add a stripe for each State our flag would now have forty-eight stripes and in place of being a banner would be a long upright band on the flag pole. Foreseeing this, the flag was changed, in 1818, back to its original proportions, Fig. 343. But many of the flags from that date up to the Civil War time had the constellation of stars grouped in the form of a star.

Figs. 340, 341 and 342 show the changes in the form of our flag up to 1818.

Fig. 341 is our first flag and our last. To the Union of our large flags, however, we add a new star for each state shown by Figs. 343 and 344.

"THE STAR SPANGLED BANNER"

This song was inspired by the sight of the great flag of fifteen stripes (Fig. 345) at that time flying over the ramparts of Fort McHenry (September 1814), when Francis Scott Key, under a flag of truce, visited the British fleet.

The circumstances under which Francis Scott Key wrote this song, as related by his daughter-in-law in 1898, is in part as follows: "My father-in-law" said the old lady, "wrote the poem—he did not think of it at that time as a song—on the back of an old letter while he was waiting on an English man-of-war for morning. He was a temporary prisoner during the night, negotiating the release of his friend, Dr. Beane, of Prince George County, Maryland.

"The next day he showed the verses that he had written to his uncle, Mr. Joseph H. Nicholson, who possessed a fine literary judgment, and he, Mr. Nicholson, gave them to Captain Edes—or I should say, he intended to—but the Captain was not in his printing office, and so the Star Spangled Banner was printed and distributed by an apprentice boy.

THE FIRST ONE TO SING IT WAS A BOY

"named Jimmey Lawrensen, who stood upon a printer's stool in the open public square and sang to the crowd."

The particular flag about which Key wrote was formerly

the private property of Colonel Armistead and descended to Eben Appleton. It was until recently stored away in a Broadway Trust Company's vaults, but it is now carefully preserved at the U. S. National Museum at Washington, where it should be and where all may see it.

According to Mr. Stewart, Key was on the Minden when he wrote the song, and in commemoration of this a "Star Spangled Banner" buoy marks the spot where the Minden lay at anchor on that occasion. The position of the vessel was determined by the Office of Library and Naval War Records, Navy Department, with the aid of Mr. William G. Perrin, Secretary of the British Navy Records Society."

The original Star Spangled Banner was made by Mary Pickerskill, under the direction of Commodore Barry and General Striker; it is about thirty feet wide by forty feet long and has lost one of its stars. Some authorities claim that this was shot away and others say that it was cut out from the flag and sent to Abraham Lincoln.

In 1812 we were still adding a stripe for each state admitted to the Union. To remedy this, Captain Reid of New York City had his wife, Mary Reid, and some of her young friends make a new flag of the original design of our first flag. This flag was first hoisted over the House of Representatives on April 13th, 1818, the U. S. Congress having on April 14th, 1818, adopted Reid's flag by passing a law that after the 4th day of July the next flag of the United States be thirteen horizontal stripes, alternate red and white, and that the Union have twenty stars, white on a blue field. "And be it further enacted," says the law, "that on the admission of every new State into the Union, one star be added to the Union of the flag and that such addition shall take effect on the Fourth of July next succeeding such admission," Fig. 343. This is the law to-day for our large flags, but our small flags of to-day still have the thirteen stripes and thirteen stars. Thirteen is a lucky number for the United States, but sometimes a bit unlucky for other nations.

THE STARS AS SYMBOLS

While our five-pointed star probably came from the rowels of knight's spurs on Washington's shield, nevertheless stars are used as symbols and the six-pointed star is the

STAR OF BETHLEHEM

The Christmas star! It is the only one which should be used at Christmas-tide, as each of its six points is supposed to be guarded by its own particular angel and the whole thing represents Egypt (the pyramid) up set and Judea (the pyramid) set firmly on its base, the combination making the six-pointed star, the Star of the East which guided the wise men to the Manger.

The five-pointed star being "irregular," has no such a symbolism and is often improperly used at Christmas-tide, but very properly used on our flag.

The unofficial American flags, however, did not all use the five-pointed stars and the writer remembers seeing many in his youth with many pointed stars, but they were home-made flags.

The Masonic Grand Lodge of Raleigh, North Carolina, has the original flag carried by the North Carolina soldiers at the battle of Guilford Court House in 1781. This old banner has thirteen horizontal stripes of alternate blue with white field for the Union Jack, spangled with thirteen *eight*-pointed stars. It is one of the freak flags and no doubt a home-made affair. To the good housewife a star was a star and the number of its points a matter of personal fancy.

THE EASTON FLAG

presented by the women of Easton to Captain Abraham Horn's Company of volunteers, is another example of the whims of the donors being worked into the banners, for this flag has the stripes for a Union Jack and a circle of twelve eight-pointed stars surrounding one central star all placed where the stripes should be.

Also many flags formerly bore an eagle on the blue field like the Fremont flag, Fig. 346, but with this difference, the eagles, as a rule, were better drawn than the funny bird on Freemont's old calumet or peace banner.

In the flags of All Nations, published in Gleason's Pictorial Drawing Room Companion, in 1854, the twenty-six stars of the American flags are shown arranged in a group forming one big star. This same design appears upon the pictures of our flag at Fort Sumter in 1861.

How Old Glory Got Its Name

The name of Old Glory was not in common usage until sometime after the war of 1861 had been fought. and the writer never heard it used until about 1880, but it hit a popular chord and is now in universal use.

According to the Salem (Mass.) News, the naming and the history of the expression is as follows:—

"Captain Driver was born in Salem, March 17, 1803. The flag which became historic while in his possession was presented to him in 1831 on the sailing from Salem of the brig Charles Doggett, which he commanded. The Civil War found Captain Driver a retired shipmaster living in Nashville.

"Despite his absence from his Northern home, he was still a Union man in sentiments, openly and staunchly espousing the Union cause, even at the outbreak of hostilities. In his own family his loyal sentiments did not awaken sympathy. Although he never feared for his own personal safety, nevertheless he trembled for his prized ensign, for all the city knew his predilections, and of the great flag, which he cherished as one of the mementos of his seafaring days, and it had flown from his windows on every public occasion during his residence in the Tennessee city. The history of the prized colors was a matter of public knowledge and every confederate in Nashville naturally felt that it behooved him personally to get possession of the flag as a prize of war. The Driver house and grounds were often searched.

SEWS FLAG IN QUILT

"Knowing that he could not keep his prized bunting by force from falling into the hands of its enemies, the crafty and resourceful master mariner, with deftness that would have done credit to the president of a sewing circle, opened up the quilt on his bed, folded his flag of 110 yards of bunting smoothly inside with one or two other relics and artfully sewed up the coverlet and quilted it again.

"It was February 25, 1862, that the Federal troops entered Nashville and the Stars and Stripes resumed their place over the State Capitol. When Captain Driver saw this he hastened home, and, ripping open the bed quilt, took his old flag out of its snug resting place and besought of the Federal commander's permission to raise the historic ensign with his own hands in place of the small but beautiful flag of the Sixth Ohio colors which had been placed there. Not only was the permission granted, but he was also given an escort to bring the flag in safety from his house to the Capitol. The old man himself raised the banner he loved so well and then, with tears in his eyes, said to the officers:—

'OLD GLORY IS UP'

" 'I have always said if I could see it float over that Capitol again I should have lived long enough. Now, Old Glory is up there, gentlemen, and I am ready to die.' "

This was the real christening of "Old Glory" so far as is known and Robert S. Rantoul says:—"Nobody seems to have come forward claiming to have applied the designation "Old Glory" to the United States flag before 1862. It is a fair assumption that the phrase was his, and we will give him the honor of inventing it.

TRAGIC END OF THE ORIGINAL OLD GLORY

The end of the history of this particular "Old Glory" is related by Mr. O. D. Blakeslee, of Company D, Sixth Ohio Volunteers, in a letter from him to the New York Sun, February 14th, 1904.

"I was a member of Ammen's brigade, Nelson's division, then the Army of the Ohio. We left our camp, 'Wickliffe,' Ky., and marched to West Point, on the Ohio River, where we took transports and sailed down the Ohio to Paducah and then up the Cumberland River for the capture of Nashville, Tenn., co-operating with the land forces advancing toward the same objective point. Nelson was anxious to get ahead and capture Nashville before the land forces. The Sixth Ohio Infantry, of which I was a member, was on the flagship with Nelson and consequently in the advance. We (the Sixth Ohio) were the first to land at Nashville, and after forming and throwing out an advance guard we marched through the streets and took possession of the Capitol building. Captain Driver appeared shortly afterward and showed us the precious relic, which he had hidden in his bed, and presented the flag to our regiment.

We carried it ever afterward in our headquarters baggage wagon, through all our campaigns toward Shiloh, the race from Alabama to Louisville, Ky., to head off Gen. Bragg; down through the battles of Stone River, Berryville, Chickamauga, Mission Ridge, Chattanooga, etc.

"Alas, the ever-present mule, the ever hungry and curious mule, in his search for grub, happened across this self-same flag and ate at least one-half of it. I well remember the sadness that fell upon us all when the fact became known. I don't know what ever became of the remnant of that particular 'Old Glory.' These are facts."

RESPECT TO OUR FLAG

Mark Twain has said that education and environment can bring a body up to believe in anything. And we know that sight stimulates imagination; imagination makes thought; thought produces action; continued action becomes habit; habit makes character!

To those of us whose hair has been blondied by the peroxide of Old Father Time, it seems strange and unnatural that any native or foreign-born citizen should be, or could be ignorant of the usual customs and etiquette connected with our flag, and yet we find this quoted from Scribner's Magazine. "I know a house where for a week or two after America's rebirth the flag was continuously displayed night and day proudly flapping *union down*. And I talked to sweet girl graduates of American schools who did not know that there was a star for every State, or that there were forty-eight; and one in particular who, when I wearily informed her that there were thirteen stripes, exclaimed: 'Thirteen! How awful!' "

REAL AMERICANS

Have no patience with such people; they look upon the parents of such girls as either criminals or dead beats who live in luxury on the wealth made possible by the freedom and liberty of a grand democracy which they fail to help, understand or appreciate. Strange to say the parents of these useless and consequently dangerous young girls, are, as a rule, of old American families, but the girls are as unfit as their parents and teachers to live in America.

But the boys! God bless them, they are always patriotic and can be relied upon in times of dire need in spite of a few disloyal school teachers, or even of the influence of "comfortable" parents, who have forgotten that it is the protection of Old Glory which has made their comfort and fashionable ignorance possible.

We Americans hate war and look upon it as an invention of the evil one. Nevertheless, we are compelled to own up that the present war has done a great work in awakening the healthy, manly spirit in us, and giving new life to the patriotism and religion sleeping in the breasts of our pleasure-loving American citizens.

It has been a rude awakening from the dope dreams of luxury, tango and feverish life of the Great White Ways, but America is now awake and the war was the alarm clock which caused her to open her eyes.

FORMS OF RESPECT TO THE FLAG

There is no federal law telling how to behave in polite society; there is nothing in the Scout law telling the boys the details of what his behavior should be, the Scout law simply says, "A Scout is trustworthy, loyal, helpful, friendly, courteous, kind, obedient, cheerful, thrifty, brave, clean and reverent." It is supposed that every Scout knows what these words mean, or will find what they mean, and it is supposed that everybody knows how to be polite, and will obey those social laws which custom gradually makes and which all people learn to observe from habit and example.

WHAT OUR FLAG REPRESENTS

There is no federal law telling us how to hang our flags and banners, but custom has already established polite usage. Our flag represents ourselves, our better selves, not only that but it represents our parents and all that was good in them, not only that but it represents the fundamentals—that is, the groundwork—of democracy and human freedom, consequently we must treat it with the greatest deference and respect.

THE LAWS OF CUSTOM

require that a flag should never be hauled to the top of the staff before unfurling it, but should fly free while being hoisted, and that it should be quickly pulled aloft.

But when the colors are lowered they should come down slowly and with dignity, as the flag approaches the ground the color guard should see that the banner itself does not touch the ground, floor or deck of a boat, ship or barge. Our flag should never be allowed to trail in water or dust, care should be taken to keep it from places where it will be soiled or contaminated.

A flag is made to fly free from a flag-staff and not to be used as a piece of decoration or draped over tables for public speakers or even the pulpits in churches.

For the purpose of decoration red, white and blue bunting should be used. Our flag should not even be festooned over door-ways and arches, it is made to fly free and has a right to fly free. The American flag should never be raised nor lowered except by hand; it should be allowed to hang straight down from its supporting rope, or wave freely from a staff or mast. When not flying it should be folded and stored away in box, trunk or chest.

It is customary when hanging the flag across the street, or when the flag is suspended from the windows of a house, to so arrange the colors that the Union Jack, that is the field of stars, is toward the north; in such streets as run east and west; but if the street in which the flag flies runs north and south, then it should be so hung that the Union Jack is at the eastern edge of the flag.

It is a grave and discourteous breach of etiquette to display the flag of one nation above any other nation with which it is at peace. National flags of many nations, when displayed, should be on separate staffs and not one above the other.

When the Colors are Lowered

At sunset while the band plays the "Star Spangled Banner," all spectators should come to attention and uncover, at the first note of the anthem. When we say come to attention, we mean that they should stand erect with their shoulders thrown back, heels together, left arm down at the side, hat in right hand held opposite the left shoulder, in this position they should remain until the last stanza of the Star Spangled Banner is played, when they resume their former attitude.

Millitary men are required to come to attention by the Army regulations, and Boy Scouts and all others in uniform should come to attention and, without removing their hats, should stand at attention facing the colors, remain at attention throughout the ceremony, but not salute until the last note is sounded after which they resume their former position whatever that may be.

CHAPTER XXIX

LIBERTY POLES

Liberty Flags; "Liberty or Death;" American Freak Flags; California Grizzly Bear Flag; Fremont's Calumet or Peace Flag; First History Written of the Texan Flag; Notes on the Confederate Flag; New York Artist Designs Confederate Battle Flag; Our War Between the States, A Family Affair Conducted Between Gentlemen; Modern German Practices Not Countenanced in the War of '61

AMERICAN FLAGS began to appear here and there before the American Revolution made it necessary to standardize the designs. Massachusetts used the pine tree standard. The armed vessels of New York sailed under a white flag emblazoned with a black beaver.

Among the first signs of unrest here was the crop of liberty poles which would spring up over night faster than the indignant British soldiers could chop them down. What made it more aggravating for the soldiers and more fun for the boys was the trick the Americans had of sheathing their "Liberty" flag poles half way up with sheet iron, and from these ironclad poles fluttered all sorts of impudent and saucy flags with irritating mottoes and designs. This accounts for the early array of freak flags used by our revolutionary patriots.

Fig. 347. Just as this book is going to press comes the announcement that at Dobbs Ferry, New York, one Michael La Vista, while remodeling an old building he owns which he is converting into a garage, found concealed in the walls of the house, an old Revolutionary flag. The standard was wrapped in a real old blue uniform coat of the Continental soldier, trimmed with buff.

233

The antiquarians and collectors, arch enemies, moths and buffalo beetles have almost destroyed the precious coat, but the flag being made of linen is still in excellent

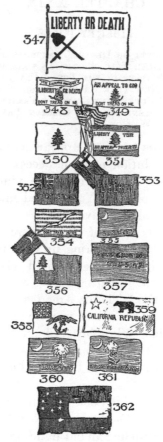

condition. By reference to the old flags we find that one of similar design was used at the battle of White Plains. This newly discovered flag measures 24x36 inches, is of white linen with inscription and design of sword and liberty cap in black. The motto is "Liberty or Death" and is from Patrick Henry's famous speech.

Fig. 348. The Culpepper, Minutemen's flag.

The Gadson flag was similar to the Culpepper but minus the scroll at the top and the motto under it of "Liberty or Death."

On February 9th, 1776, Colonel Gadson presented to Congress "an elegant" standard, such as is to be used by the commander and Chief of the Navy. This was a bright yellow flag, its centre having an awesome picture of a rattlesnake coiled and ready to strike. The motto below was, "Don't tread on me." This flag met the approval of Congress. Legend says that the color of this flag was suggested by the yellow Quarantine flag of Great Britain, which was yellow with a black plague spot in the center occupied by the equally deadly rattlesnake in the American flag.

Fig. 349. About the first legislation in the Continental Congress relating to flags was that of October 18, 1775, when several cruisers were equipped and set sail under the pine tree flag, Fig. 349. It is claimed by Cooper in his life of Paul Jones that the flag flown by Paul Jones was the combination of the Pine Tree and the rattlesnake, but in this he is apparently mistaken.

Fig. 349. Flag of the Massachusetts Privateers.

Fig. 350. The Pine Tree Flag.

Fig. 351. Another form of the Pine Tree Flag carried by the Colonists.

Fig. 352. Tautons Flag.

Fig. 353. Flag used at battle of Long Island.

Fig. 354. Flag used from July 4th, 1776, to July 24th, 1777. First Navy Jack.

Fig. 355. Fort Moultry Flag, which flew from the southeast bastion of Fort Sullivan (Moultry) in Charleston Harbor, June 28th, 1776. It was this blue flag with a Crescent that Sergeant Jasper so gallantly rescued when its staff was shot away and the banner fell outside the walls of the fort. The troops wore blue uniforms with a crescent on their caps inscribed with, "Liberty or Death."

Fig. 356. The Bunker Hill Flag. Continental flag 1775-1777.

Fig. 357. Is the famous blue battle flag of Commodore Perry.

Fig. 358. The Regimental Flag of Rhode Island, white silk with 13 stars on a blue field; a blue anchor surmounted by a blue scroll inscribed with the word "Hope." It was carried at Brandywine, Trenton and Yorktown, and may still be seen at the State House at Providence.

Fig. 359. The Grizzly Bear Flag of California.

FLAG OF CALIFORNIA

According to Lafayette F. Norman, a veteran of early California days, it was in 1846 that the Americans of that State grew tired of Mexican rule and held a meeting at Sonora, where they declared their independence, adopted a constitution and a flag, the latter consisting of a grizzly bear painted upon a piece of bunting.

The revolution was really known as the Bear Flag Movement and was largely due to friction between Captain Fremont and General Castro of Mexico. When Captain Fremont visited California with his famous exploring expedition in 1846, the Bear Flag was hoisted. This happened after Ezekiel and thirty-two Americans captured Sonora on June 14, 1846. The Bear Flag in the hall of the Daughters of the Revolution, at Washington, D. C., has a red stripe on its lower edge, the bear is on a white field.

FREMONT'S FLAG

Fremont's flag had an odd arrangement of stars in two string-like beads one over and one below a queer sort of bird, meant to represent an eagle. But since arrows are a sign of war with the Indians and since the American eagle always has a clawful of arrows, Fremont had a calumet, or Peace Pipe, put in with the arrows so as not to stir up the war spirit among the redmen with his banner.

TEXAN WAR FLAG

The author has received a letter from the State Librarian of Texas, informing him that a flag designed by his father, James H. Beard, N. A., for a company of Kentuckians in the War of Independence of Texas, is preserved at the State Capitol.

In the War for the Independence of Texas, Congressman David T. Disney of Cincinnati, a connection of Mr. Beard's family, furnished the filibusters from that city with arms and two brass cannons which were smuggled at night aboard a steamer bound for New Orleans. A company of volunteers was formed in Newport, Kentucky, and as they were not countenanced by the government they could not use the American flag. But since they desired a banner of some description, they appealed to James H. Beard, the artist, to design one for them. The young pioneer artist complied with their request and painted a Goddess of Liberty on a blue silk ground (if I remember aright), with the old motto "Liberty or Death."

As the volunteers were marching thru their native town a lady threw her glove, which a gallant young Kentuckian picked up, kissed and then placed on top of the flag staff, where it remained throughout the war. The surviving Kentuckians brought back with them the flag which won the independence of Texas, tattered and torn, but with the little glove still resting proudly on the staff, altho it too showed the marks of battle.

Both flag and glove are now preserved in Texas, altho the artist who designed it, the Kentuckians who fought for it and the Kentucky girl who threw the glove, have all long since hit the trail over the Great Divide, where all the pony tracks point one way, and even the incident of the flag is not known to the people of Texas itself, as their State librarian has informed the author. It is put down here in detail so that the history of this flag will not be relegated to fableland with Betsy Ross and the unrecorded flags.

In the War of 1861 the only Confederate flags which we on the border saw in use, or captured trophies, consisted of three stripes; red, white and red with a blue square in the upper left-hand corner containing thirteen white stars in a circle. One of these flags I have before me as I write; it was captured at Fort Cotton by Company I, of the Thirtieth Missouri regiment, under command of Captain Harry Beard, U. S. A.

THE HAMPTON FLAG

Fig. 360. A blue flag with the word "Hampton" and a crescent and palmetto tree stenciled in white, made from a water-color sketch by the author from the original flag, sketch was made while on a southern sketching trip.

Fig. 361. One more blue flag drawn from memory of a flag used in South Carolina in 1861.

THE MERRIMAC FLAG

Fig. 362. The flag which flew from the peak of the famous Confederate ironclad, Merrimac, was similar in design to the Fort Cotton flag, previously mentioned, but the Merrimac flag drawn from photograph has, however, only seven stars.

The Ensign of the Confederate Ironclad Albemarle

Captured by Lieutenant W. B. Cushing, in 1864, was the "Stars and Bars" design with thirteen white stars on the X cross. Near the close of the war the writer saw the troops coming in thru Kentucky with captured Confederate colors consisting of the battle flags known then as the stars and bars, said to be originally designed by one of our New York artists and illustrators.

Origin of the Stars and Bars

Lieutenant R. M. Shurtleff, of the 99th New York Volunteers, U. S. Coast Guard, so the story goes, while out scouting a short time before the first battle of Bull Run was badly wounded and captured by the Confederates. He was kindly treated by them, but as there were no military prisons at that time he was put in the poor house at Richmond, Virginia. The story of the designing of the stars and bars was told in New York many years ago.

It seems that Shurtleff while still weak from the effects of his wound and unable to walk about spent much of his time reclining on his cot and making drawings for the amusement of himself and the Confederate soldiers.

The Confederate officers became interested and secured paints and brushes for him. One day one of the officers who had been particularly kind to him said, "I wonder if you could design a sort of patriotic emblem for me." "I might," replied the prisoner, smiling, "but I suspect that your idea and mine of what a patriotic emblem is wouldn't be quite identical." "Very likely not" agreed the other, "but this isn't anything that you need trouble your conscience about. Gen. Beauregard's little daughter is a great chum of mine and I promised her I'd get up some sort of painting of a Confederate flag for her to hang on the wall. I've been trying to think up something, but as a designer I'm no use. So, it occurred to me that you might help me out." "Why, of course, I'll be glad to do what I can," said Lieutenant Shurtleff. "Give me a few days' time and I'll get something done in water colors."

Getting out his paints he set to work to sketch and presently, with the instinct of the artist, became deeply absorbed in the matter of the design, working all that day and getting up early the next morning to continue the task, discarding one idea after another until he finally hit upon a design that suited him. This was the St. Andrew's cross in blue on a red ground, with minor ornamentations of stars. He finished it up handsomely in water colors and turned it over to his Confederate friend who was much pleased with it and brought back word that little Miss Beauregard was highly delighted and was going to importune her father to let the Yankee gentleman who had made it go back North. Shortly after Lieutenant Shurtleff was transferred to Libby Prison and in 1862 was exchanged. He forgot about the design for the time. A year or so later it was called to his attention in rather a startling way as he saw a captured Confederate battle flag consisting of his design almost exactly as he had painted it. Still later he saw an official flag of the Confederate States of America, and there was another repetition of the design, for it formed the entire corner of the ensign. Naturally, the artist was not pleased with his friend, the Confederate officer, who had put him in the position of furnishing flag designs for the people he was fighting.

From what he has learned since, however, it seems that the officer was not in fault. It appears that Gen. Beauregard saw the painting which had been given to his daughter and on asking her about it was told that it was the flag of her country and belonged to her personally. He suggested that she present it to her country and after some consideration she agreed, stipulating that the original be returned to her after copies had been made. The flag was then reproduced in cloth and Gen. Beauregard had it adopted as the battle flag of the Confederacy. Just how it came to be incorporated into the official flag Lieutenant Shurtleff does not know. At the close of the war the Southern Association of Veterans adopted the original battle-flag design for their button.

The War of the States was a family affair of our own. It was what might be called a personal affair, and it was a war between GENTLEMEN. There was none of the terrible deeds committed then that are of daily occurrence now.

For the benefit of people who were not themselves in the war zone, I want to say, that the author himself saw a Union soldier in a Union camp strung up by the thumbs for speaking disrespectfully to a woman on the street, and he has been told of even harsher treatment used by the Confederates for similar offenses. This incident is told so that the boys of America will know that the present horrible practices adopted by Germany were not countenanced in our country even during the bitterest part of our civil conflict, and most of the German outrages were unknown to us even by name. Thank God, women and children are still safe in America.

CHAPTER XXX

SIGNS SHOWN BY TRAILS, TRACKS, TRACES AND SPOOR OF ANIMALS

ANIMAL SIGNS

THE signs animals leave on the trail are, as a rule, unintentional except with such creatures as possess odors peculiar to themselves. These animals possibly in all cases, certainly in many cases, use the odor as a signal to other creatures of their own kind.

The fox, wolf and dog are conspicuous in this line and the fact that all old trappers use different sorts of "scent" with which to doctor their traps prove in a measure that other animals, such as the beaver for instance, also recognize their own family odor, for the castor of the beaver, that is the scent glands of the male animal, are used by all trappers for "doping" the traps set for these wary creatures.

But men, as a rule, follow the signs unintentionally left by the wild creatures, such as their dropping or their tracks in the mud, dust or snow. The nibbled branches of the bushes, the torn bark of the striped maple or moosewood, tell where the moose has been, and the freshness of these marks unmistakably tell us whether the creature was there recently or not. The bull also leaves the marks of his horns on the trees where he rubs them after the manner of the domestic cattle.

When the snow covers the ground in winter the tracks of the moose are often nearly obliterated by snow falling after the animal has passed, but even when the trail is but a series of slight depressions in the snow the real woodsman can tell the direction travelled by the moose, and this

242

he does in true Sherlock Holmes style. He knows that such animals (and man too for that matter) when walking in the snow strike the latter with a forward slide of the foot, this of course packs the snow at the toe end of the track but leaves it loose at the heel where there is only a downward pressure, consequently when these tracks are old and only marked by a series of depressions, the wise old woodsman takes a stick and by prodding the tracks with it easily discovers at which end the snow is packed and hard (probably also frozen) and knows that that is the direction travelled by the animal.

BEAVER TRAILS

The beaver leaves his trail even in the water, for where he feeds and works the water is full of poplar, birch, elder and willow sticks neatly cut and with all the bark peeled off by the sharp chisel-like teeth of the animal, also there may be found floating the potato-shaped roots of the yellow water-lily on which are the unmistakable marks of the beaver's teeth, showing where he has been lunching. The marks of the beaver's teeth on these roots are more distinct than the marks made by the teeth of a small boy on a half eaten apple.

BEAVER HOUSES

Besides the houses built of sticks, like giant muskrat houses in the still waters of the beaver lakes or ponds, these animals pull the brush up on the banks of running streams; plaster mud over it and live in holes in the bank beneath the brush, while in front of these "bank houses" is a circular mass of sunken food sticks approximately twelve or fourteen feet in diameter.

Inasmuch as the smaller branches of the sunken sticks protrude above the water, these caches of winter's food make conspicuous signs along the edge of the river telling even the novice or tenderfoot that Mr. and Mrs. Beaver's winter home is located on the bank at that spot.

BEAVER DAMS

The most remarkable sign of the beaver is their scientifically constructed dams by means of which they secure still water so that their food supply will not be washed away by the current. While on a moose hunt in Northern Canada last month, in one forenoon we had to portage or force our canoes over six of these dams.

BEAVER SLIDES

Evidently the beaver thinks he has nothing to conceal but himself for the muddy slides on the shore, where he hauls the logs and brush down to the water, are as conspicuous as the "slipperies" made by the boys on the steep muddy banks of the southwestern streams, for the purpose of coasting down into the water on summer days.

TREE SIGNS

On the shores of the beaver-inhabited lakes and streams large birch, balsam and poplar trees are felled by the beaver, all the trees falling towards the water, but this is accidental and not planned by the little animals, as my recent investigation proved to me. The trees in a forest all lean towards the light which in this case is the open water and the trees fall in the direction they lean.

I have seen trees two feet in diameter neatly cut down by the beaver. Their presence in a stream or lake is immediately apparent to any visitor, altho he may not see a single animal, for these creatures seem to be utterly indifferent about concealing their presence, altho very careful about concealing themselves, so that one rarely sees a live beaver and in one month's travel thru their lakes and dams. altho we could hear them at any time of night splashing in the water where they were feeding in front of our camp, we only saw three of them in the daytime.

BEAVER SIGNALS TO EACH OTHER

The beavers slap their tails on the water as they dive as a signal, that it is time for the others of the tribe to disappear. They also make this same signal when at play, but probably with the same meaning, that is, even in play it is a signal to vanish. Only last month the author heard the beaver splashing around in front of his camp, all night long as they played and fed on the roots of the yellow waterlily or splatter-dock.

ANIMAL SIGNALS

Everyone who has visited the old West, or even only attended a performance of the Wild West Show, know that the blat of a horse is a sign of trouble for the rider; it is the vicious cry of an "outlaw" or that of an unbroken range horse when first it feels the saddle on its back. The neigh of a horse is the sign of a friendly greeting to fellow horses, a sort of hello or howdy sign, and the low whinny is a sign of gentle contentment or a pleading for oats or a lump of sugar. An angry horse sometimes squeals like an angry bull elk.

BUFFALO OR BISON

A buffalo or bison bull's sign of defiance is a deep vibrating bellow, but the bison cows and calves when they are angry, make a noise more like a blat than a bellow. They come at one with the hair on their backs standing

up, like the hair on the back of an angry elk. The herd
of six hundred bison which at one time occupied Horse Plains
in the Flathead reservation, once charged the author as
he was attempting to photograph them and he had a rare
opportunity of noting their behavior.

MOOSE

The moose has a rather prolonged roar or bellow followed
by a shorter one and ending with a low grunt, as a sign
that he is ready to meet all comers in battle and contest
with them for the title of the boss moose of the range.
The bull will also rattle his antlers against a limb or tree
making quite a loud noise thereby, and Mr. Andrew J. Stone,
the famous Northland hunter told the writer that natives
ofttimes call the bull by rattling a stick on an old horn or
another stick.

I have heard the moose at night rattle their antlers
on something, presumably a tree or branch, and have had
them answer my very imperfect imitation grunts while
I was seated in front of the camp fire feeding on a fine juicy
steak of one of their fellows. One writer spells the bull's
grunt—"oh-ab" and the moo of the cow moose "moo-
waugh-yuh" but no spelling can represent the real sounds
which are as weird, wild, peculiar as is the form and meat of
the moose itself.

Indeed it does not seem necessary to make a good imitation of a moose call in order to get a reply, for they will
sometimes come at the sound of the lumberman's axe as it
thwacks the tree, at the sound of the involuntary cough of
the hunter as he stealthily creeps thru the forest and even
at the report of his gun when he fires.

Recently the writer shot a big bull for meat; the bull, accompanied by two long-eared big cow moose, stood on the

shore facing him one hundred yards distant. With the report of his gun the great animal crumpled up and fell in the edge of the water. But the cows stood their ground even when we paddled up to within fifteen or twenty feet of them, and they even refused to leave when we waved our canoe paddles almost in their faces. Not only did they decline to be frightened, but they followed us up and down the shore for a quarter of an hour with the hair on their tall shoulders bristling like that on the back of an angry dog.

Moose tracks are like those made by oxen, but more vigorous and incisive.

ELK

Not only does the elk squeal, but it also raises the hair on the nape of its neck and gnashes its teeth as a sign of anger. The elk, like the common deer, gives a whistle as a signal of warning. The writer has often come suddenly on a buck deer and seen it scamper away displaying the "White Flag" of the Deer Clan, only to circle around some distance away, face the intruder and bugle its warning as a sign to all other creatures that man, the dreaded enemy of all forest folks, was near. The "white flag" is the widely spread tail which flashes in the woods suddenly upon one's sight and is most disconcerting to the hunter, as it is probably intended to be. The author has more than once failed to shoot because he mistook the white flag for a man in his shirt sleeves. The "white flag" means retreat and is a sign of safety first with the Virginia deer.

THE PRONG-HORNED ANTELOPES' MYSTERIOUS CODE OF SIGNALS

All the old-time big game hunters of the West have noticed the two white patches on antelopes. Those spots are used as signals which can be read by the other antelopes, which have eyes to see or noses with which to smell. Even such animals as are devoid of acute sense of smell can read the visual message which the antelope gives to warn his friends of danger.

The hairs on the rump patches are long, white and ordinarily point downward. Among the roots of the hair is a gland which secretes a strong musk. Underneath the skin at this point is a broad sheet of muscles which have the power to raise these hairs so that they stand out at all angles like "the petals of a huge white chrysanthemum." When an antelope sees danger this muscle acts and the patch flashes out like snow. In the middle of each is a dark-brown spot, the musk gland, which frees a great quantity of the musk, which can be detected down the wind for a long distance by another antelope. Even man with his blunted sense of smell can detect the oder of this danger-signal for some yards.

It is claimed that the antelope has five different sets of glands, each giving forth a different kind of musk for use in its daily life as a means of getting or giving intelligence. The use of the two in the middle of each rump patch has been explained, but the purposes of the others have not yet been fully accounted for and their use is as mysterious as is that of some of the so-called perfumes used by the ladies.

COYOTE'S SIGNAL

According to my old friend Buffalo Jones, the coyote's call of distress is four short yelps followed by a long howl. This, Colonel Jones says, means that Mr. Prairie Wolf has his foot in a trap or that he has lost his mate. The writer is more or less familiar with the yap, yap, yap of the coyote when it sits behind a stump or stone and acts the ventriloquist by making the sound of a whole pack of prairie wolves, but he has not had the opportunity of years of living with these wild dogs as has his friend Colonel Jones. The latter is quoted as saying that, when the coyote sounds his danger-signal he (the Colonel) knows that it is time for him to take his rifle, call the dogs, and get ready to kill a lion. It is the coyote's cry for help. It is always used when a coyote runs across a mountain lion and the cry is taken up and sent on by every coyote who hears it. Sometimes it is used when danger is threatening the young, and on such occasions it never goes unanswered.

Jones further says, that the call of distress is entirely distinct and pitched in a different key. When danger threatens two shrill yelps are given, followed by a pause and four quick yelps. The distress, or SOS call is made up of four short yelps, followed by a long drawn howl. It means one of two things—that a coyote has lost his mate or that he is trapped.

The food call is described as being joyous, enthusiastic, and continuous, as it should be, and embraces the whole vocabulary of the coyote language, barks, yelps and howls, all mixed up in one and the general effect is indicative of keenest pleasure and anticipation. All who have camped in the western wilds have heard this call. Colonel Jones says that he has often sounded the call himself, and it brought up every coyote in hearing distance, already licking its chops. The hunger call has the same intermingling of noises, but is tuned in sorrowful cadence. At least so says my friend the Colonel; personally I have never been able to understand coyote language, altho I have heard them "talk."

The crow has one caw or rather a ka-r-r-ah, which

it uses as a cry of warning and all the wild creatures understand the signal and disappear. I have seen a dozen gray
squirrels while at play suddenly scamper to their holes
when the old sentinel crow sounded the warning that a man
was near.

A pack rat and a rabbit stamp their feet in anger. A
common brown rat will make a noise like tut, tut, tut, as
a threat and a gray squirrel scolds by making a noise which
sounds like cud-joe, cud-joe.

Most of the signals among beasts are signs of danger,
anger, affection or calls for food. For instance, the growl
or purr of the cat tribe, the growl and bark of a dog or
fox, the bellow of a bull, the bleating of sheep and all the
noises of the farmyard are familiar examples of animal
talk to be heard at the end of the day.

A CATALOG OF SELECTED
DOVER BOOKS
IN ALL FIELDS OF INTEREST

A CATALOG OF SELECTED DOVER
BOOKS IN ALL FIELDS OF INTEREST

ABC BOOK OF EARLY AMERICANA, Eric Sloane. Artist and historian Eric Sloane presents a wondrous A-to-Z collection of American innovations, including hex signs, ear trumpets, popcorn, and rocking chairs. Illustrated, hand-lettered pages feature brief captions explaining objects' origins and uses. 64pp. 0-486-49808-5

ADVENTURES OF HUCKLEBERRY FINN, Mark Twain. Join Huck and Jim as their boyhood adventures along the Mississippi River lead them into a world of excitement, danger, and self-discovery. Humorous narrative, lyrical descriptions of the Mississippi valley, and memorable characters. 224pp. 0-486-28061-6

ALICE STARMORE'S BOOK OF FAIR ISLE KNITTING, Alice Starmore. A noted designer from the region of Scotland's Fair Isle explores the history and techniques of this distinctive, stranded-color knitting style and provides copious illustrated instructions for 14 original knitwear designs. 208pp. 0-486-47218-3

ALICE'S ADVENTURES IN WONDERLAND, Lewis Carroll. Beloved classic about a little girl lost in a topsy-turvy land and her encounters with the White Rabbit, March Hare, Mad Hatter, Cheshire Cat, and other delightfully improbable characters. 42 illustrations by Sir John Tenniel. A selection of the Common Core State Standards Initiative. 96pp. 0-486-27543-4

THE ARTHUR RACKHAM TREASURY: 86 Full-Color Illustrations, Arthur Rackham. Selected and Edited by Jeff A. Menges. A stunning treasury of 86 full-page plates span the famed English artist's career, from *Rip Van Winkle* (1905) to masterworks such as *Undine, A Midsummer Night's Dream,* and *Wind in the Willows* (1939). 96pp.

0-486-44685-9

THE AWAKENING, Kate Chopin. First published in 1899, this controversial novel of a New Orleans wife's search for love outside a stifling marriage shocked readers. Today, it remains a first-rate narrative with superb characterization. New introductory note. 128pp. 0-486-27786-0

THE CALL OF THE WILD, Jack London. A classic novel of adventure, drawn from London's own experiences as a Klondike adventurer, relating the story of a heroic dog caught in the brutal life of the Alaska Gold Rush. Note. 64pp. 0-486-26472-6

THE CARTOON HISTORY OF TIME, Kate Charlesworth and John Gribbin. Cartoon characters explain cosmology, quantum physics, and other concepts covered by Stephen Hawking's *A Brief History of Time.* Humorous graphic novel–style treatment, perfect for young readers and curious folk of all ages. 64pp. 0-486-49097-1

A CHRISTMAS CAROL, Charles Dickens. This engrossing tale relates Ebenezer Scrooge's ghostly journeys through Christmases past, present, and future and his ultimate transformation from a harsh and grasping old miser to a charitable and compassionate human being. 80pp. 0-486-26865-9

CRIME AND PUNISHMENT, Fyodor Dostoyevsky. Translated by Constance Garnett. Supreme masterpiece tells the story of Raskolnikov, a student tormented by his own thoughts after he murders an old woman. Overwhelmed by guilt and terror, he confesses and goes to prison. A selection of the Common Core State Standards Initiative. 448pp. 0-486-41587-2

Browse over 10,000 books at www.doverpublications.com

DOOMED SHIPS: Great Ocean Liner Disasters, William H. Miller, Jr. Nearly 200 photographs, many from private collections, highlight tales of some of the vessels whose pleasure cruises ended in catastrophe: the *Morro Castle, Normandie, Andrea Doria, Europa,* and many others. 128pp. 0-486-45366-9

DUBLINERS, James Joyce. A fine and accessible introduction to the work of one of the 20th century's most influential writers, this collection features 15 tales, including a masterpiece of the short story genre, "The Dead." 160pp. 0-486-26870-5

ETHAN FROME, Edith Wharton. Classic story of wasted lives, set against a bleak New England background. Superbly delineated characters in a hauntingly grim tale of thwarted love. Considered by many to be Wharton's masterpiece. 96pp. 0-486-26690-7

FLATLAND: A Romance of Many Dimensions, Edwin A. Abbott. Classic of science (and mathematical) fiction — charmingly illustrated by the author — describes the adventures of A. Square, a resident of Flatland, in Spaceland (three dimensions), Lineland (one dimension), and Pointland (no dimensions). 96pp. 0-486-27263-X

FRANKENSTEIN, Mary Shelley. The story of Victor Frankenstein's monstrous creation and the havoc it caused has enthralled generations of readers and inspired countless writers of horror and suspense. With the author's own 1831 introduction. 176pp.
0-486-28211-2

THE GARGOYLE BOOK: 572 Examples from Gothic Architecture, Lester Burbank Bridaham. Dispelling the conventional wisdom that French Gothic architectural flourishes were born of despair or gloom, Bridaham reveals the whimsical nature of these creations and the ingenious artisans who made them. 572 illustrations. 224pp.
0-486-44754-5

HEART OF DARKNESS, Joseph Conrad. Dark allegory of a journey up the Congo River and the narrator's encounter with the mysterious Mr. Kurtz. Masterly blend of adventure, character study, psychological penetration. For many, Conrad's finest, most enigmatic story. 80pp. 0-486-26464-5

THE HOUND OF THE BASKERVILLES, Sir Arthur Conan Doyle. A deadly curse in the form of a legendary ferocious beast continues to claim its victims from the Baskerville family until Holmes and Watson intervene. Often called the best detective story ever written. 128pp. 0-486-28214-7

HOW TO DRAW NEARLY EVERYTHING, Victor Perard. Beginners of all ages can learn to draw figures, faces, landscapes, trees, flowers, and animals of all kinds. Well-illustrated guide offers suggestions for pencil, pen, and brush techniques plus composition, shading, and perspective. 160pp. 0-486-49848-4

JANE EYRE, Charlotte Brontë. Written in 1847, *Jane Eyre* tells the tale of an orphan girl's progress from the custody of cruel relatives to an oppressive boarding school and its culmination in a troubled career as a governess. A selection of the Common Core State Standards Initiative. 448pp. 0-486-42449-9

JUST WHAT THE DOCTOR DISORDERED: Early Writings and Cartoons of Dr. Seuss, Dr. Seuss. Edited and with an Introduction by Rick Marschall. The Doctor's visual hilarity, nonsense language, and offbeat sense of humor illuminate this compilation of items from his early career, created for periodicals such as *Judge, Life, College Humor,* and *Liberty.* 144pp. 0-486-49846-8

THE LADY OR THE TIGER?: and Other Logic Puzzles, Raymond M. Smullyan. Created by a renowned puzzle master, these whimsically themed challenges involve paradoxes about probability, time, and change; metapuzzles; and self-referentiality. Nineteen chapters advance in difficulty from relatively simple to highly complex. 1982 edition. 240pp. 0-486-47027-X

LINE: An Art Study, Edmund J. Sullivan. Written by a noted artist and teacher, this well-illustrated guide introduces the basics of line drawing. Topics include third and fourth dimensions, formal perspective, shade and shadow, figure drawing, and other essentials. 208pp. 0-486-79484-9

MANHATTAN IN MAPS 1527-2014, Paul E. Cohen and Robert T. Augustyn. This handsome volume features 65 full-color maps charting Manhattan's development from the first Dutch settlement to the present. Each map is placed in context by an accompanying essay. 176pp. 0-486-77991-2

THE METAMORPHOSIS AND OTHER STORIES, Franz Kafka. Excellent new English translations of title story (considered by many critics Kafka's most perfect work), plus "The Judgment," "In the Penal Colony," "A Country Doctor," and "A Report to an Academy." A selection of the Common Core State Standards Initiative. 96pp. 0-486-29030-1

THE ODYSSEY, Homer. Excellent prose translation of ancient epic recounts adventures of the homeward-bound Odysseus. Fantastic cast of gods, giants, cannibals, sirens, other supernatural creatures — true classic of Western literature. A selection of the Common Core State Standards Initiative. 256pp. 0-486-40654-7

THE PICTURE OF DORIAN GRAY, Oscar Wilde. Celebrated novel involves a handsome young Londoner who sinks into a life of depravity. His body retains perfect youth and vigor while his recent portrait reflects the ravages of his crime and sensuality. 176pp. 0-486-27807-7

PRIDE AND PREJUDICE, Jane Austen. One of the most universally loved and admired English novels, an effervescent tale of rural romance transformed by Jane Austen's art into a witty, shrewdly observed satire of English country life. A selection of the Common Core State Standards Initiative. 272pp. 0-486-28473-5

RELATIVITY SIMPLY EXPLAINED, Martin Gardner. One of the subject's clearest, most entertaining introductions offers lucid explanations of special and general theories of relativity, gravity, and spacetime, models of the universe, and more. 100 illustrations. 224pp. 0-486-29315-7

THE SCARLET LETTER, Nathaniel Hawthorne. With stark power and emotional depth, Hawthorne's masterpiece explores sin, guilt, and redemption in a story of adultery in the early days of the Massachusetts Colony. A selection of the Common Core State Standards Initiative. 192pp. 0-486-28048-9

SKETCHING OUTDOORS, Leonard Richmond. This guide offers beginners step-by-step demonstrations of how to depict clouds, trees, buildings, and other outdoor sights. Explanations of a variety of techniques include shading and constructional drawing. 48pp. 0-486-46922-0

TREASURE ISLAND, Robert Louis Stevenson. Classic adventure story of a perilous sea journey, a mutiny led by the infamous Long John Silver, and a lethal scramble for buried treasure — seen through the eyes of cabin boy Jim Hawkins. 160pp. 0-486-27559-0

WORLD WAR II: THE ENCYCLOPEDIA OF THE WAR YEARS, 1941-1945, Norman Polmar and Thomas B. Allen. Authoritative and comprehensive, this reference surveys World War II from an American perspective. Over 2,400 entries cover battles, weapons, and participants as well as aspects of politics, culture, and everyday life. 85 illustrations. 960pp. 0-486-47962-5

WUTHERING HEIGHTS, Emily Brontë. Somber tale of consuming passions and vengeance — played out amid the lonely English moors — recounts the turbulent and tempestuous love story of Cathy and Heathcliff. Poignant and compelling. 256pp. 0-486-29256-8